WAYS TO SAY
I LOVE YOU

To Those You Love the Most

Stephen Arterburn, Carl Dreizler
& Jan Dargatz

Published in 1994 by BBS Publishing Coporation.
Inspirational Press edition published in 2006

Inspirational Press
A division of BBS Publishing Corporation
450 Raritan Center Parkway, Edison, NJ 08837

Inspirational Press is a registered trademark of BBS Publishing Corporation.

Published by arrangement with Thomas Nelson Inc., Publishers

Distributed by World Publishing
Nashville, TN 37214
www.worldpublishing.com

Library of Congress Control Number: 93-80401

ISBN: 0-88486-384-0

Printed in the United States of America.

Contents

I. ❤ Simple Ways to Say "I Love You"

❤ Contents

❤ Introduction

Throughout the pages of this section are simple ways to tell the important people in your life how much you love them. Some of the ideas are new. Some of them are as old as mankind itself. Our hope is that you will pick up this book and use it to say "I love you" in many different ways.

Just saying "I love you" is not enough, for loving someone is not merely saying the right words. The best way we can say "I love you" is to spend increasing amounts of time with the people we love. Most of the ideas presented here provide you with ways to say you love someone and to confirm that love through time together.

We've purposely written each idea so that almost all of them could be used by any two people who love one another. Husbands and wives. Mothers and daughters. Fathers and sons. Lifelong friends. Use these ideas with your grandparents. Grandchildren. Family. Friends.

If your goal, however, is to create more sparks in your romance with someone, each of these ideas can lead to that end. This section will teach you to have lots of fun in any loving relationship. We hope it will also help you gain the respect of people close to you. And because they will see you as a fun and loving person, you will probably feel lots better about yourself.

Look through the ideas. If you've always found it hard to say "I love you," start with one idea that doesn't seem too threatening. Try it out. Then move on to another idea. Before long, you may find yourself thinking of your own new ways to say "I love you."

You should never run out of ways to express your love for someone. You can use some of these ideas time and time again. And you can add your own personal touches to the suggestions included.

We hope this book will be a useful tool for building a stronger bond with the important people in your life. From the lonely neighbor next door or the son you never seem to find time for to your relationship with the person you love most, we are convinced you can grow stronger together.

1 ♥ Moonlight Walk

How wonderful to walk a mile
In the morning or at noon
But he or she will like your style
If that walk's beneath the moon

The Idea: Talk about a simple idea! Yet how often have you purposely taken a walk under a full moon? This idea is especially appropriate for those who are in a relationship where romance is a factor. If you want to woo your sweetie, this one's for you.

Yet, this idea is appropriate for any two people who love each other. Even for those nonromantic relationships with loved ones, there's still something magical about a walk in the moonlight, something that makes the heart more tender and willing to express feelings.

Planning Your Walk: This event needs little planning. In fact, it can be done on the spur of the moment. Look outside tonight. If the moon is full, drop everything, grab the one you love, and find a quiet, open spot away from the crowd.

If you want to plan your moonlight stroll, find out when the next full moon will be. Go a step further, and find out what time the moon is rising and setting. You can find this information by checking your local newspaper or by calling either your local weather bureau or public library.

Selecting Your Setting: While you always have the option of walking beneath the moonlight near your home, the best moonlight walks take place where there are wide-open spaces. You're lucky if you live near a desert. In the mountains, search for a place that overlooks the lower elevations. In the winter, seek a place where the moon will reflect off newly fallen snow.

If you live near a large body of water, time your walk so you can see the moon rise or set above it. There's something beautiful about moonlight shining on a body of water.

What to Say: We don't need to tell you what to say. That will take care of itself. There's something about a full moon. . . .

2 ♥ The Retreat

Pack a lunch and get away
Your life should not be dull
Leave the dishes one more day
The office in-box full

The Idea: Because our weekends or other days off become as hectic and filled with chores as the days we work or go to school, we must plan special days with friends and loved ones. Why not say "I love you" by setting aside one full day to go away with the one you love for a time of reflection and introspection?

This event should not take place as part of a company picnic or during a day you were planning at the beach or park for some other occasion. This day should be scheduled solely for the purpose described below. This retreat is recommended for two people rather than groups or entire families.

Preparing for the Big Day:

1. Pick a place that is special to the two of you. While it is difficult in many parts of the world to find totally isolated spots, try to make this your primary goal. Perhaps you know of a hiking trail in the mountains, an isolated beach, a cabin in the wilderness, or a stream in the woods.

2. Set the date with the one you love.

3. Review the "Reflections" sample included in this section. Feel free to alter the sample and produce your own final copy. Make two copies of your Reflections sheet. Write your name in the blank space at the top of the sheet you will be giving to the one you love. Write the other person's name in the blank for the Reflections sheet you will keep. Put these and two or three pens in an envelope. Don't forget to take the envelope with you!

A Suggested Schedule for Your Day:

8:00 a.m.   Pack a picnic lunch with your favorite snacks and beverages. It might be fun to splurge on this one and use the picnic basket rather than brown paper bags. But since this is a day of rest and relaxation, use whatever you want.

9:00 a.m.   Say goodbye to everyone else who isn't going and head out the door.

10:30 a.m.   Arrive at your special place. Take a walk, talk, and just enjoy being together. But don't get into topics to be discussed later. Maybe you'll want to hold hands (if appropriate). This is the warming-up period, a time to enjoy the serenity of your new environment. If you or your partner have a hard time leaving work and worries behind, here are two ideas that might help:

- *Pick up a rock. While holding it in your hands, speak to the rock, saying, "I am placing all the stress of my job, my finances, my relationships and everything else into you today. This is my day to relax. Hope you enjoy your day holding all these burdens for me just as I will enjoy mine without them." Toss the rock far from you, thereby releasing all your worries—at least for this day.*

- *Breathe deeply. Move your head in slow, easy circles about your neck. Shake your left arm as a way to represent one thing on your mind that you want to clear out for the day. Do the same thing with your right arm to release another distraction. If you've got more, shake both of your legs.*

12:00 p.m.   Find a relaxing spot and eat lunch. After lunch lie down on your backs and look straight up into the sky or at the branches above you if you happen to be under a tree. Talk about what you see. Talk about your thoughts.

1:30 p.m.   Explain to the one you love that you each will go to separate places for the next two hours. Pick an easy spot to find for your reunion at about 3:30. Tell your companion to think about your relationship since its inception as you both walk to your separate private places. Before parting, give the other person the appropriate Reflections sheet and a pen. Ask him or her to complete each thought with a sentence or paragraph before you rejoin. You do the same.

3:30 p.m.   Meet at your agreed-upon spot. Share with one another what you have written. Look him or her in the eyes as you read. Try to be tender.
You may want to alternate reading your responses to the Reflec-

tions items or have one person at a time read the entire sheet.

5:30 p.m.   Walk together for a half hour reflecting silently on what just happened. Try not to talk during this last part of your day.

6:00 p.m.   Hug the one you love and tell that person you love him or her. Your special retreat is over.

Reflections

Complete each thought with a few sentences expressing your deepest feelings about_____.

The first time I met you . . .

I first knew I loved you when . . .

My favorite memory with you is . . .

My favorite thing about you is . . .

The thing I've always wanted to tell you but never have is . . .

My favorite part of this day with you has been . . .

The promise I make to you today with regard to our future is . . .

3 ♥ Are You Interested?

Find the interest they like most
Something you have never done
Take the hobby that they boast
You just might have some fun!

The Idea: I'm sure your loved one has a hobby, interest, or pastime that you have always thought was a waste of time or was something you would never want to do. Well, it's time you mount that dirt bike or search for that red bird with the yellow bill, if only for a day or two.

In every relationship both parties should have activities they like to do on their own. It's healthy to have separate and individual interests. But showing an interest in someone else's favorite pastime, if only in a limited way, is an expression of love. So begin now to plan a day for the two of you (or for the family) to do that special hobby together.

Preparing for the Big Day: The first thing you need to do is sit down and think about all the hobbies and interests of the one you love. List five of them here:

_____

_____

_____

_____

_____

Now rank them by putting a 1 in front of the hobby he or she would be most shocked to see you take part in, and a 5 before the item he or she would find the least shocking. Now, you decide which activity you will participate in. Will you pick the one you can most tolerate, or the one the other person would never, in a million years, expect you to do?

Announcing Your Interest: You have at least two options here.

> 1. Tell the one you love to reserve a day for something special, and make it a surprise when you tell him that morning you will be joining him for a day of deep-sea fishing.

> 2. If you want to make the shock less dramatic, you can tell the person what you have in mind when you set up the date initially. This may be the courteous thing to do if you want to make sure you have picked her favorite beach for skin diving.

Compounding Your Interest: You may choose to make this a low-key event or go all out. Here are some ways to make the day even more memorable:

- Buy or borrow the outfit that is typical for this hobby, and greet your friend all decked out in your special clothes. If you are going bird watching, buy the red and black flannel shirt, special pants, and inventory book. Oh, and be sure to have your binoculars around your neck.

- If you really want to make the day special, invite all his buddies or her girlfriends to go, saying that you just want to be one of the gang.

- Read up on the hobby or interest so you will sound as though you know what you are talking about.

Above all, enjoy yourself!

4 ❤ Hour Class

Today before they go away
Put a note inside the shower
But don't just give them one today
Write them one for every hour

The Idea: Imagine receiving not just one message of love from someone, but a message an hour for one full day. Here's the idea. One selected morning, give the one you love a stack of envelopes. On the front of each one will be the time of day, one envelope for each hour from 7:00 a.m. to 10:00 p.m. That's sixteen envelopes in all.

Inside each envelope will be special messages of love written by you. The person you love will open one each hour as marked. This idea may be one of the simplest and yet most memorable ones of the fifty-two in this book. Try it.

Selecting the Right Day: This idea is best suited for a working day or some other time when you will not be with the one you love. The notes may have more meaning when you are not around. And the one you love may be more anxious than ever before to see you at the end of the day.

Going the Extra Mile: For a little added fun, slip some small gift into a few or into all of the envelopes. Use photos of the two of you or of others in your life whom you both love. Hand write a certificate good for a romantic dinner with you. Insert a piece of chewing gum. Include a picture drawn by one of your children. Put lipstick on your lips and then kiss a piece of paper.

Preparing Your Messages:

You can implement this idea on any budget. You can write your notes on lined paper and use business envelopes or go all out and buy sixteen different greeting cards. You can also use personal stationery to make each note look the same or use a variety of things to make each package as different from one another as possible.

Plan your notes wisely, perhaps saving the most sentimental and deeply felt messages for the hours closest to your getting together that evening. Here are some ideas for various times throughout the day. These are notes from Bob written to his wife, Ann.

7:00 a.m.
(Placed in the shower or near the bathroom sink)

Ann, by the time this day is over, I want one thing to be perfectly clear in your mind—the fact that I love you. After you take your shower and get ready for work, pick up the stack of envelopes I put near your briefcase. Open each one only at the time marked on the outside of the envelope. I'll be thinking about you as you open them. Have a fun day.

12:00 p.m.

By now you should be having lunch. I wish I could be there to eat with you. Remember the day we had the picnic down at Little Falls? That was the first day I knew I really loved you. I still do. I've enclosed a piece of gum as a treat for you when you finish eating. Enjoy it.

5:00 p.m.

If you're like me right now, you probably thought this day would never end. Come on home. I'll have dinner waiting for you. It's your favorite. I've enclosed a cartoon I saw in the Sunday paper. Maybe it will give you something to smile about as you drive home.

10:00 p.m.

This may be the last note of this special day, but it certainly will not be the last time I tell you how much I love you. Come and see me right now. I'll tell you in person this time. Good night. You're a very special woman.

5 ♥ Love Defined

Love is patient; Love is kind
Though no two define it the same
Take this example and see what you find
Replace the word "love" with your name

The Idea: What better way to show your love for another person than by evaluating your own ability to display love. What a difficult word *love* is to define. Perhaps the best description of love is found in the New Testament book of First Corinthians:

Love is patient
Love is kind
It is not jealous
Love does not brag
And it is not arrogant

Love does not act unbecomingly
It does not seek its own way
It is not provoked
Love does not take into account a wrong suffered
It does not rejoice in unrighteousness
But rejoices in truth

Love bears all things
Believes all things
Hopes all things
Endures all things

Love never fails*

* 1 Corinthians 13:4–8, paraphrased from the New American Standard Bible.

Assessing Yourself as One Who Is Loving: One genuine way to say "I love you" is to work on becoming a person who is more loving with each day. Try the following exercise as regularly as you can, *especially* when life gets tough and you don't feel as though you are as loving as you could be.

Take the above definition of love, and insert your name everywhere the word *love* or its pronoun appears. Let's use someone named Ken as an example:

> *Ken is patient*
> *Ken is kind*
> *Ken is not jealous*
> *Ken does not brag*
> *And Ken is not arrogant*
>
> *Ken does not act unbecomingly*
> *Ken does not seek his own way*
> *Ken is not provoked*
> *Ken does not take into account a wrong suffered*
> *Ken does not rejoice in unrighteousness*
> *But rejoices in truth*
>
> *Ken bears all things*
> *Believes all things*
> *Hopes all things*
> *Endures all things*
>
> *Ken never fails*

Is it possible to pass all of these tests? Of course not. Especially the last one. We all fail in one way or another every day. But the goal is to use this model to analyze how well you love. Use it often. Then work on the areas where you fall short.

Any improvement you make in yourself tells the ones you love how much you care about them.

6 ♥ Sunrise, Sunset

You find yourself all over town
Your days, they just go by
But stand and watch the sun go down
You'll stop and wonder why

The Idea: Whenever we take time out of a busy schedule to sit in a favorite spot and watch the sun complete its day, we often wonder why we work so hard, why other things take precedence over this simple experience. Most of us could watch the sunset every night for the rest of our lives and never get bored.

If your favorite place to watch a sunset happens to be a place where other people go to view the same phenomenon, observe them next time you go. Just before sunset, people will stop walking, stop talking, and simply gaze at the sign from God that another day has ended.

Make watching the sunset a common event with the one you love. Each day as you watch the sun go down, say, "I love you." We never really know if we will be there when the sun sets tomorrow.

Reviewing Your Day: Every day that you watch the sunset with people you love, take a few moments to find out how their day went. We often don't take time to ask such simple questions as, "How was your day?" Nor do we take the time to listen to the responses. Here are some other suggestions for your conversations with loved ones at the end of a busy day.

- Thank each one for something he or she did for you today.
- Ask what you can do to be more support-ive.
- Tell a special someone you are glad to be sharing the sunset with him or her.
- Share something for which you are grateful to God.
- Ask what their favorite part of the day was.
- Encourage them in any trials they may be facing.
- Tell them how much they mean to you.
- Say, "I love you."
- Invite them to watch the sunset with you tomorrow night, too.

An Alternative: If you and the one you love are both early risers, or if evening schedules prevent sunset viewings, try finding a special place to watch the sunrise. Instead of reviewing the day and seeing it come to a close, reflect on the promises each new day provides. Spend part of your time listening to the new day beginning. Start the new day by saying, "I love you." Few things can ruin any day that begins with these three words.

7 ♥ Carin' Valentine

Guess it all comes down to this
The day that's made for love
For first romance or marital bliss
Just thank our God above

The Idea: For Valentine's Day, you probably have a lot of your own ideas. But here are some suggestions to make the day that was made for love even more special.

Making the Next Valentine's Day the Best Ever:

- *Make the largest Valentine card* you can imagine. Find a refrigerator carton, paint a heart and Valentine message on it, and then stand it up in your living room on Valentine's Day.

- *Put a message in front of your house* using a real estate sign with cardboard taped over the realtor's information. Instead write "Inside this house is the most wonderful wife in the world. Her name is _____."

- *Instead of buying candy this year,* make the candy yourself, and then give it to the one you love. Don't worry if it looks homemade. The effort you took will mean more than the candy's appearance.

- *In addition to sending roses* or instead of sending roses, bring them home with you. If you live in a place where flowers grow year-round, go together to a place where you can walk and pick your own bouquet.

- *Buy Valentine's Day cards,* not just for the most significant person in your life, but for other people who may never receive Valentines.

8 ♥ Plan a Treasure Hunt

Check the tape deck, push rewind
Do what you are told
You're the treasure they will find
Who needs silver or gold?

The Idea: This idea is lots of fun. You will be a pirate who has buried a treasure and has recorded its whereabouts in code. The one you love is the lucky explorer who finds the clues leading to the secret treasure—and the secret treasure is you!

It might be fun for two or three couples to implement this idea together. The husbands can be the pirates, the wives the explorers. Or you may want to have your whole family participate, or perhaps a group of friends.

Planning Your Treasure Hunt: First, set a date with the one you love, explaining that he must leave your house, or not arrive there, until a specified time that you designate. Tell him he must be prompt, but not early. Your loved one will be thinking you have planned a wonderful surprise party and will expect people to jump out and hug him when he enters the house. Instead, he will find an empty house and the first of many clues leading to the "buried treasure."

Much to your friend's surprise, he will not find an old treasure chest filled to the limit with jewels, gold, and silver. Instead, you will be seated at a favorite restaurant, waiting with a fresh bouquet of flowers or tickets to a play you both have been wanting to see. How romantic.

The Treasure Hunt: Here's where you can use your imagination. Carefully plan a series of ten to twelve clues, each of which leads to the next and the last of which leads to you! But you're going to need an escape hatch—just in case your clues are too clever. You don't want to be stranded in some romantic restaurant, sitting alone with wilted flowers.

To solve this dilemma, and to help you get started, we've provided a suggestion for your first note, which must be placed where the other person is sure to find it. Be sure he has a way to get into the house. Remember, he's expecting you to be there.

CLUES TO THE SECRET TREASURE

Congratulations! You have just found the first clue that, if followed correctly, will lead you to a secret treasure. Begin your treasure hunt as soon as you read this note, or you will miss out on a great opportunity!

But First, A Word of Caution

> If this puzzle gets too tough,
>   no treasure have you found.
> At eight o'clock be by the phone,
>   'cause I want you around.
> I'll tell you where the treasure is,
>   and where you have to go.
> But try to solve this simple game;
>   the first clue is below.

CLUE #1: Look into my ice.

You'll find the location of Clue #2 there.

(If you can't figure this out, look at the back of this paper. But try to solve the clues on your own.)

On the back of Clue #1 you would write, "Clue #2 is in the freezer." This is again to ensure that you don't get stranded. If you think the one you love is clever enough to figure out your clues, don't bother with the easy answers.
     Proceed with all your clues until the final one tells how to get to the restaurant where you are located. It might read something like this:

CLUE #12:

There's a restaurant down the street,
the one where we like to eat.

The address is Two Two Four Nine Three
that is where the treasure'll be.

Again, if you think your clue will seem unclear, write
the name of the restaurant on the back. Once there,
the one you love can celebrate the victory of finding
the "buried treasure" by spending an evening with
you.

Dry Run: Before you leave the house, do a dry
run to make sure you left the clues in the right order.
Is this one of the more simple ideas in this book?
Nah! But it's so much fun we had to put it in!

9 ❤ Put Another Candle On

The one you love is one year older
Their bones may start to creak
So this year plan events much bolder
Celebrate all week

The Idea: This year instead of celebrating only the actual birthday of the one you love, celebrate the entire preceding week!

Planning a Week-Long Birthday Celebration: Here are a few ideas to get you started.

Count down the days until his or her birthday. One week before the birthday, and on each day thereafter, start a countdown by giving the person you love a card or by placing a big sign somewhere in the house (such as on the refrigerator or on the car windshield) saying "Seven more days until your birthday!"

Ask a different friend or family member to surprise the person on each of the countdown days. Tell each person you contact that he or she is responsible for doing something special (along with you) for the one you love. The seventh day prior to the birthday may be a good time for the people at work to throw some kind of surprise lunch. The sixth day may involve your loved one's two best friends, who greet the person as he or she is leaving work for the day. And so on.

Give the person you love a gift each day. Even if you don't have a big budget, you can give gifts that have some special significance each day. You may want the gifts to relate to each other, such as different parts of a new outfit or different tapes of the person's favorite music.

Throw a surprise party. You may want to throw a surprise party on day four or five. Because you are doing all these other crazy things, the person might expect a surprise party on the exact birthday. This will catch him or her off guard.

Make the actual birthday day extra-special in some way. Because you have prepared all these different surprises throughout the week, you don't want the actual birthday to be a letdown. So end the birthday week with a nice dinner between the two of you or with the family, bestowing your final gifts and perhaps presenting a scrapbook of the week's events.

When the person you love goes to bed on that birthday night, he or she will know at least two things: you don't forget birthdays, and you love him or her very much!

10 ♥ Singin' in the Rain

*Next time your plans are
    altered
Because of sudden rain
Don't let your day be faltered
The sunshine's loss, your gain*

The Idea: Are you disappointed when a free day is spoiled by an unexpected rainstorm? Don't allow it! Remember as a child how much fun it was to go out in the rain? You would find the deepest puddles to splash in. You may have dropped a leaf in some gutter filled with rushing water and followed it down the block until it disappeared into a drain. Now you can make the best of a rainy day with the one you love.

"But we might get wet!" you say. That's the point. If you don't get wet, this idea may not be any fun at all. Put on your raincoat, your galoshes, and a hat.

Ways to Have Fun When the Weather Gets Dreary:

Plan a picnic lunch. You don't have to eat *in* the rain, but find a covered patio in a nearby park. Everyone has picnics in the sunshine. You'd be surprised how much fun it is to do things that are out of the ordinary.

Reenact your favorite movie scene in the rain. Perhaps the most memorable rainy movie scene was Gene Kelly's famous walk and dance down the street while he was crooning, "Singin' in the Rain." Or the gazebo scene from "The Sound of Music." Find a gazebo. You may feel you are "sixteen going on seventeen" again.

Take a walk in the rain. This is the simplest idea yet within this category. Just grab an umbrella and take a walk arm-in-arm. It might just bring you closer emotionally than you've been in a while.

Regress to childhood. Take the one you love outside in the rain and find the deepest puddles. See who can splash the most water on the other. See who can roll down the hill the farthest. Put on some old clothes. Abandon your adulthood, and just get wet!

View the storm. Find a special place to view the storm. If you are near the ocean, sit in a restaurant overlooking the stormy sea. If it's a thunderstorm, find a place with a view so you can watch this amazing phenomenon. If you are too tired for anything else, just build a fire and gaze out the window together.

11 ♥ Home, James

Gather up your loved one's friends
Get a chauffeur's hat
Where you go it all depends
On where they want you at

The Idea: Give the one you love a day or evening with friends. You don't even have to treat them to anything. Just offer to be their chauffeur for the afternoon or evening.

Here's the plan. Just tell the one you love (wife, husband, daughter, son, or anyone else you love) that you want him or her to select two or three friends (depending on the size of your car) for an afternoon or evening of fun. The agenda is theirs, although you might suggest they plan several stops for the evening so they can take full advantage of your services. Otherwise, you may be bored, sitting in the car for hours while they attend a double feature or sit through a three-hour concert.

Things You Might Need: The following are suggestions of what you might need to make this event a success. As with other suggestions in this book, you may choose to be as simple or as extravagant as you want, depending on how much money you have and how much time you want to spend planning the event.

The car. You have quite a few options here.

The simplest solution is to use your own car, as is. Or you may want to pretend it's a limo by putting a small flag on the antennae and a sign on the back that says "limo." A middle-of-the-road option is to use a friend's Lincoln or Cadillac for the evening. If you want to go all out, there are classic car rental agencies in some cities that will rent a limo for the evening.

The Outfit. At the simple end of the scale, wear a dark suit or skirt and jacket with a white shirt and black bow tie. If you want to go all out, rent a tuxedo.

Perhaps you can find some white gloves. In any case, you've got to get one of those black hats chauffeurs wear in the movies.

The Equipment. Whether you are in your own car, a friend's car, or a rented car, you can stock up the back seat with goodies found in a limousine (as long as you follow the law, of course). Start with an ice bucket containing a chilled bottle of sparkling water or cider. Of course you must have some fine stemware glasses for serving purposes. Cheese and crackers might be a nice touch too. If you have access to one, set up a battery-operated television set. Beyond these, use your own imagination to make the ride classic and memorable.

Etiquette. Always open the doors for your passengers. Offer them your hand for getting in and out of the car. Call the ladies "ma'am" and the gentlemen "sir." At each stop, clean up the back seat, replacing used glasses with new ones. Pick up and drop off each passenger at their place of residence. Change your name to "James."

12 ❤ When You Wish upon a Star

Ask the person you love most
Three things they're wishing for
If one's a villa on the coast
Forget that, there's two more

The Idea: There's a wonderful organization named "Make a Wish" that makes dreams come true for kids with terminal illnesses. What a great way to say, "I love you." This idea is based on the same principle. Wouldn't it be nice if you could help make a wish come true for someone you love? Give it a try.

The genie in the lamp. Simply ask the one you love, "I'm curious to know what you would want if you were told you had three wishes?" To be creative, find an old lamp and give it to the one you love. Include a card with the above question. If he or she makes wishes that are not possible to fulfill, such as "I wish for ten million dollars" or "I wish for a life with no illness," ask him or her to think of things that are within reason.

You may want to respond by telling them three special wishes you would make and leave it at that. You wouldn't want the one you love to suspect your ulterior motives.

Your wish is my command. Your goal, however, is to select one of the wishes and make it come true.

If possible, try to make all three dreams come true. You may fall short because of your budget or other constraints. Just do your best.

For example, if one wish involves going to Hawaii some day, start a savings account especially for the trip. If Hawaii is out of the question, surprise the one you love some weekend by taking him or her to some place you can afford. You might say, "I couldn't make your Hawaii dream come true, but because I love you I wanted us to get away for a few days anyway. Keep dreaming. Some day your wish will come true."

13 ♥ Yuk, Yuk

If together you give
Lots of love and laughter
You just may live
Happily ever after

The Idea: Laughter is one of the more important ingredients to a lasting relationship. Find things to do with the one you love that make you laugh. When schedules get too busy or life is too stressful, find something to do that makes you both howl.

Laughing It Up: Below are some suggestions for tickling your funny bone.

>*Rent your favorite comedy movie.* Go to your nearest video store and rent a movie that makes you both laugh. There's bound to be one or two movies that will tickle your funny bone time and time again.

>*Get out or purchase your favorite funny book.* Books by humorists and gifted cartoonists abound. If you look hard enough, you will find one that parallels your sense of humor. When you find a book that makes you laugh, save it and share it with the one you love.

>*Look at your old yearbooks* or old photographs. Seeing the way we looked years ago or read-

ing what someone wrote in our yearbook can often be the best entertainment around. Show someone who has only known you in recent years a picture that is ten, twenty, or thirty years old. If they don't laugh, they're probably being polite.

Go hear a comedian or two at a local comedy club or other place of entertainment near you. If there are no such places around, many professional comedians have made videos you can rent.

Just laugh! Sometime when you are sitting with someone you love or a group of people you love, just start laughing. Try to laugh harder and harder with each passing second. If two or more people begin laughing for no apparent reason, the laughter can become contagious. You may soon find yourself in a roomful of people who are laughing hysterically for no apparent reason. Keep it up. Few things are better for you than a good laugh.

14 ♥ Just Kidding

Find a carousel to ride
Or jump a rope instead
You can find the kid inside
It's all within your head

The Idea: Be kids for a day. Experience puppy love or that special camaraderie that is so characterized by childhood friendship. Do you become more dull and boring with each year? It doesn't have to be that way. Kids have ways of being and doing whatever they feel like at the moment. They seldom think, until they reach adolescence, "what will people say if I do this or that?" We as adults are all too concerned that someone may see us do "something childish." Why is that so bad?

Planning Your Day: Think of things little kids do that adults don't do very often. Observe your own kids, nieces and nephews, or grandchildren. See what playful things they do during a typical day. Then plan your day around childhood play. You may want to invite some children along to help you lose your inhibitions.

Selecting Activities:
- Build sandcastles.
- Run after the ice cream truck.
- Ride a merry-go-round.
- Visit a zoo.

- Play hopscotch or jump rope.
- Make drawings with crayons or water colors.
- Play with clay or Play-Doh.
- Roll down a hill.
- Visit a playground. Swing, go down the slide, get on the teeter-totter.
- Play hide and seek.

Making Your Day Even More Fun: Try dressing up like little kids. Put your hair in pigtails or braids. Give everyone a lollipop or go out for an ice cream cone.

You may just discover old love can find youth again!

15 ♥ Home, Sweet Home

Why go out and run around?
Just stay at home alone
You control the mood and sound
Just disconnect the phone

The Idea: How many times have you put aside an evening together with someone you love, only to have it spoiled by a telephone call that changes your plans. This may be the most inexpensive and simplest idea in this entire book.

Setting the Stage: To enjoy your evening at home, you will need to do a little planning. Here are some things to consider.

> 1. If you and the one you love are husband and wife and you have children, find a babysitter who will take the children to her house. Instead of leaving the house to find some peace and quiet, you send away the noise and find peace and quiet within your own walls.

> 2. Set a specified time to get together. And stick to it. Don't let delays cut into your time at home together.

> 3. Decide that you and the one you love will

run all the errands and do all the chores that day before your specified meeting time. If anything didn't get done, you both agree to let it go for the evening.

4. Make a list of any supplies you might need. Food for the meal, if you're eating together. Wood for the fire. A new tape for the stereo.

5. Set the date with the one you love.

Making the Most of Your Evening: Here are some additional ways to make the evening special.

1. UNPLUG YOUR PHONE. If the babysitter must have a telephone number, give your next door neighbor's (be sure your neighbor is home). He or she can alert you if there's an emergency. Aside from that, nothing should disturb your time together.

2. If the season is right and you have a fireplace, light a fire. Even if your companion for the evening is a child, a good friend, or a close relative, a fire adds warmth to the mood as well as to the room temperature.

3. Play some quiet music that will add to the serenity. For this particular evening leave the heavy metal music in the closet. Your purpose tonight is to talk, laugh, and enjoy each other.

4. Think of some activity you both enjoy doing

(other than watching television or a movie—these deter conversation).

5. Spend at least some time during the evening talking with each other. Take this planned opportunity at home to get to the heart of your love for each other. Evenings focused on someone else make that person feel special. And loved.

16 ♥ What Anniversary?

Celebrate times that are special to you
On the dates that would always be
*   missed*
The one thousandth day since you
*   first said "I do"*
Or the one hundredth time that you
*   kissed*

The Idea: Surprise the ones you love with special celebrations on days that will catch them completely off guard. Most of us remember anniversaries, birthdays, and other special events on the annual date that corresponds with the event's first occurrence.

For example, if your daughter was born on February 4, you always celebrate her birthday on February 4. But how can we surprise our loved ones with special days they are not even aware of?

Planning Special Surprises and Anniversaries: Here's how the idea works. Let's say Jim and Andrea were married on August 23, 1988. They would expect to celebrate their marriage on August 23 of every year thereafter. But what if on May 23, 1991, Jim were to come home with flowers, a gift, and an anniversary card. Andrea's first thought might be, "Jim forgot the month of our anniversary."

But Jim may be wiser than Andrea thinks! For Jim is actually celebrating the one-thousandth day since their wedding. Andrea had no idea that this milestone was coming. She is moved. And good old Jim is the greatest thing that ever happened, just because he sat down and made a few quick calculations.

The one-thousandth day celebration: In the above example, here's how we figured the approximate date.

Year one	365 days
Year two	365 days
Subtotal	730 days

Then we take the 730 and subtract it from 1,000 to see how many days into year three is the one-thousandth day.

1,000	days
−730	days
270	days

Next, if we figure there are an average of 30 days in each month, we divide the 270 days by 30 and arrive at a figure of exactly 9 months into year three. So if you add two years and nine months to the wedding date or any other significant event in your loved one's life, you will come within a few days of their 1,000th anniversary. Celebrate it!

If you've known the one you love a very long time, use similar steps to approximate your five-thousandth day together. Or your ten-thousandth!

Other Suggestions: Use the same idea for other events. If you are an employer and you love your employees enough, surprise them on the one-thousandth day since they joined the company. Here are a few other unusual days on which to surprise friends and loved ones:

- The seventh month (year), seventh day (month), and seventh hour (day) since you went on your first date with a special some-one.
- Plan a celebration of the first time your now-accomplished son or daughter, niece or nephew, played in a piano recital, joined Little League, or learned to read.
- Call an old school friend you haven't seen in five, ten, or even twenty years.

17 ♥ Complimentary Copy

Compliments don't come our way
Quite enough these days
Try to find the heart to say
"You're great" in many ways

The Idea: You can say "I love you" almost every time you see someone if you sincerely compliment him or her in some way. Compliments need not be directed only at appearance. People love to hear others say something nice about their sense of humor, work, or talents. Try to compliment the ones you love at least once a day.

Thinking about Compliments: You may want to affirm and compliment those you love in these areas:

- The way they dress
- Their genuine concern for others
- Their way of always making you laugh
- Their hospitality
- Their kindness
- Their sincerity
- Their cooking
- Their ability as mother
- Their ability as husband
- Their hair
- The outcome of some chore or project they completed

Turning the Tables: What about the times when you receive a compliment rather than giving one? Accepting kind words from people is another way to say you love them. By disagreeing with their compliments, you may be hurting their feelings. Learn to say thank you and give compliments in return. Have you ever caught yourself saying things like

> *"Thanks for washing the car.* [sarcastically] *I can't believe you took time out of your precious schedule to do it."*

Perhaps instead you could say,

> *"Thank you for washing the car. I don't think I've ever seen it look so good."*

When someone says, "You look so pretty today," do you say something like

> *"Oh stop. My hair's a mess, and my dress doesn't fit right."*

Perhaps instead you could say,

> *"Thank you, you're looking pretty fine yourself."*

In all your relationships with the people you love, work on encouraging their quality traits and on accepting the praise they give you in return.

18 ♥ A Day of Servanthood

*Stay with your loved one from
  morning 'til night
Do special things 'long the way
Then if you do well your loved one
  just might
Act as your servant some day*

The Idea: Designate a day when you will be your loved one's servant from the moment he or she wakes up in the morning until time to go to bed. You really have to be committed for this one. Think of all those things you do every day that you wish someone would do for you. Well, you will be fulfilling that wish for the one you love.

Items You Might Need: Although this day could take place without any props or additional items, you can have as much fun as you want with ideas such as these:

- Give the one you love a bell so he or she can ring it every time your services are needed.

- Find a maid or butler outfit and wear it throughout the day.

- Prepare a servant's kit filled with things like tissues (to clean glasses or to offer for their nose as needed), a pillow (so you can make the person comfortable when seated), or a glass (to keep by their side so you can offer sparkling water regularly). You could also plan to serve special refreshments throughout the day.

Planning Your Special Day of Servanthood: Tell the person in advance about the day so he or she can think about what to have you do. Or, if that idea scares you, simply tell the person to reserve the day for something special. You can reveal your servanthood status as you begin your day together.

Enjoying Yourselves: Have fun with this one. Don't limit your servanthood duties to the obvious, such as serving breakfast in bed or bringing in the morning paper. Think again about those daily chores *you* hate doing.

- How many men enjoy shaving? If the one you love is a man, shave him, barber style, that day. Organize his ties by colors or patterns. Shine his shoes.

- If the one you love is a woman, brush her hair. Give her a manicure. Polish her briefcase or mop the kitchen floor.

Going the Extra Mile:

- If you like the bell idea mentioned earlier and want to give a memento of the day, have the bell engraved with your loved one's name and the date.

- Invite others in your family or group to help you in your role of servant. The more people involved, the more fun you can have. (And the less work you'll have to do!)

- Crown the one you love as you begin your day. Make him or her feel like a king or queen, well deserving of your servanthood commitment.

- If he is the one who usually takes out the trash or she the one who always cleans the bathroom, extend your day of servanthood by saying you will do those chores each day or week for the next month.

19 ♥ I Do, I Do

Reenact your wedding day
Renew the vows you made
If you're single there's a way
To thank the friends who have stayed

The Idea: This idea might seem most appropriate for married people, but it can be altered to fit any relationship. We suggest you renew the vows you made to one another if you are married. If you are not married or you want to renew vows to family members or friends, we have provided suggestions for doing that.

Saying "I Do" Again: Many different times and circumstances call for a renewal or recognition of commitment to another person. Below are a few suggestions.

- *Renew your wedding vows every year on your anniversary.* This idea is great for those who are new in their marriage and may not have enough years under their belt to conduct a full reenactment of the ceremony. Try making a tradition of this event. Get out your wedding ceremony and recite the promises you made to each other on that first day God joined you together. It might help you refocus on priorities that have gotten cloudy.

- *Reenact your wedding day.* If you've been married for several years, pick your next major anniversary as the day you will reenact your wedding day. Perhaps you still live near the place where the wedding was held. Go there. If not, conduct the ceremony right in your own backyard or in your home. It doesn't have to be a fancy affair.

  The two of you may want to do this alone. Or you may want to include your immediate family. Invite the original wedding party if you like. If you're the type of person who likes to throw a party, invite everyone you know!

- *Renew your commitment to your children.* Parents can set aside a special day when each child is thirteen or sixteen or after high school graduation. You might share with the child your love and confess your shortcomings. Ask your child to forgive you for those times you have blown it.

- *Recognize close friends in a special way.* Perhaps you have no one with whom to renew vows, but you may have a few loyal friends whom you want to recognize. Issue them a Covenant of Friendship, and thereafter celebrate their friendship each year on the anniversary date of your promise. The document might look something like this:

A Covenant of Friendship

Our world has ways of recognizing and celebrating marriages, births, and other family relationships. But few people take the opportunity to celebrate some of the most treasured people in their lives: our best friends.

this certificate is presented to

[Nathan Valypoulos]

BY HIS FRIEND _____

ON THIS _____ DAY OF _____

NINETEEN HUNDRED AND NINETY _____

I hereby covenant to be your friend until the day I die.

20 ♥ Flower Power

*Nothing's more simple, Nothing's
    more right
Than flowers delivered by you
Do it today; do it tonight
And do it one week, maybe two*

The Idea: For centuries the gift of flowers has
been the most practical and sentimental way for one
person to express his or her love for another. We
send flowers for birthdays, anniversaries, or when a
friend gets a promotion at work. We even send flowers during the tragic times of life. Whatever the occasion, the implied message is still, "I love you, and I'm
thinking about you today."

Just watch a group of women in an office try
to sit still when a delivery person brings in a bouquet
of flowers. Almost every one of them will ask herself,
"I wonder who they're for?" or "Who could be sending me flowers?" (Why do we use the example of
women in an office receiving flowers? Because not
enough women have made the move to send a man
flowers!)

Using Flowers to Say "I Love You":

- The most obvious way of using flowers is to
  send a bouquet to your loved one's home
  or office. Delivering the flowers yourself is

even more special because you are there to see your loved one's reaction.

- Consider bringing flowers home every night for one week.
- Take a walk with your loved one and pick wildflowers. Create your own bouquets.
- On special birthdays, use flowers in unique ways. For example, if it is your loved one's thirtieth birthday, have a different person present a rose and a special note every fifteen minutes throughout the day. Finally you arrive with rose number thirty.
- Send flowers to people in your office, friends, or church members who may never have received flowers before. Let them know they are loved too.
- Adopt a code using certain flowers. For example,

A rose means "I love you."

A daisy means "let's play."

A pansy means "I'm thinking about you."

A daffodil means "I'm sorry."

21 ❤ Prime Time

Try this one for seven days
Do not turn on the set
Use this book or your own ways
Make this your best week yet

The Idea: The reason television executives call evenings prime time is because this is the part of the day when most Americans are gathered around their television sets. What would happen if you, and everyone else in your house, promised to leave the television off for one full week? What are you going to do with all that time?

Why not spend it with the ones you love! Children spend as much time in a year in front of the television as they do in front of teachers. Many adults spend even more time than their kids in front of the set. So why not make time to talk, play, and listen to each other?

So Now What Do We Do?   The following is a suggested schedule for your seven days without television.

Day 1: Take a walk together and plan what you're going to do with the time you would normally be watching television. If you have children, bring them along too. Let them be a part of the planning process.

Day 2: Play games together. If you don't like card games, then bring out the board games. Scrabble. Monopoly. Clue. Do a crossword puzzle together.

Day 3: Make a surprise visit to one of your close friends, perhaps a neighbor or someone you know who may need company.

Day 4: Build a fire in the fireplace or hold your own private barbecue in the backyard. Just spend time enjoying each other's company.

Day 5: Work together on some project around the house or run some errands that you need to get done. Be active.

Day 6: Turn to one of the other ideas in this book and say "I love you" in that way.

Day 7: Make this day a day of rest. Relax around the house, go to the park and lie in the grass, or visit the beach or a nearby lake. Then come home and just talk. Discuss with one another how much time you were able to spend together instead of watching TV. You'll soon realize how "prime" time can truly be!

22 ♥ Food for Thought

Focus a day 'round every meal
Eat breakfast, a lunch and a
dinner
We're not really sure how you will
feel
But it certainly won't be thinner

The Idea: Most of our socializing with the ones we love is done during mealtimes. This idea suggests that you take one full day and plan to have three very special meals with the one you love.

Planning the Venue: Good food is important, but the settings for your meals together need careful attention. Here are some suggestions.

Breakfast

- Serve breakfast in bed.
- Go to the place in town that serves the best brunch.
- Make waffles with a choice of a dozen different toppings.
- Buy Alpha Bits cereal and spell "I love you" on the plate or in the bowl.
- Eat breakfast at a place where you can enjoy the morning view.

Lunch

- Plan a picnic lunch and find a private spot at the beach or in the woods.
- Take the one you love out for lunch and have close friends waiting there to join you.
- Order pizza and have the cook spell "I love you" with pepperoni.

Dinner

- Find the most romantic place you can for dinner.
- Have a candlelight dinner at home.
- Have friends come over and serve you dressed like maids and butlers.
- Go out to your favorite restaurant.
- Splurge on dessert.
- Eat somewhere where you can watch the sunset.

An Added Note: In many households throughout the United States, families seldom eat one meal together in a week, let alone three meals together in a day. This way to say "I love you" could not only focus on one day with three special meals, but also on the suggestion that you try to eat meals with the one you love and members of your family as often as possible—even if it means reworking some schedules.

23 ♥ Gone Fishin'

Vacation time! Let's rant and rave
But where? That will depend
On how much money you can save
And how much you don't spend

The Idea: We all need time away from our daily routines to be with those we love. One of the best ways to tell someone that you love him or her is to plan a vacation together. Even if you don't have vacation time available in the immediate future, set the time now. Half the fun of a vacation is planning and anticipating a special trip.

Considering a Budget: You don't have to have an enormous budget to plan a vacation. In fact, some of the most relaxing vacations are those close enough to home so that travel costs are low, yet far enough away that you feel removed from everyday pressures.

If you don't have any money for a trip, set your vacation far enough in the future to allow time to save the money you'll need. Set a savings plan you can stick to.

Picking the Location: Gather together all the people who will be going on the trip. Next, keeping in mind the budget constraints you've already established, use a map to explore location possibilities.

If you are on a limited budget, you may just need a map of your state or the surrounding states. If you have a more generous budget, you may want a map of the United States. And if you are one of those rare people for whom money is no object, get out a map of the world.

Developing a Preliminary Plan: Together, complete a plan similar to the following outline. As the date of departure gets closer, you can give the plan more detail.

VACATION PLAN
for

_____

(list names here)

Date of Departure: _____   *Return:* _____

Destination:

_____

Mode of travel:

_____

Route:

_____

Lodging or camping accommodations needed:

_____

One activity each person would like to do during this trip:

Name	Activity for this trip
_____	_____
_____	_____
_____	_____
_____	_____
_____	_____
_____	_____
_____	_____

24 ♥ Write It Down

Grab some paper, grab a pen
Write a special note
Say you think that she's a "ten"
Or pin it to his coat

The Idea: Who can say they don't like getting a note from someone with the words *I love you* written on it. (Maybe some of you macho people out there don't think it's cool to *write* such a note. But admit it. How do you feel when someone sends *you* a note that says "I love you"?) For many people writing "I love you" is much easier than saying it.

Saying the "Write" Thing: Of course, the easiest thing to do would be to go to the stationery store and find a gushy, sentimental card designed for a special occasion. But don't wait for a special occasion. Try this idea on the spur of the moment.

Your goal for one particular day will be to find as many ways as possible to write the words, "I love you." Here are just a few suggestions to get you started.

- Write your I-love-you note on the mirror in the bathroom with toothpaste.
- Let the grass grow thick and tall and then mow the words I LOVE YOU with the lawnmower.
- Take the one you love to the beach and write "love letters" in the sand.

- Slip a note in the cereal box so that it comes out as the cereal is poured.
- Put a big "I love you" sign *inside* the refrigerator.
- Write "I love you" in bold black letters on the tenth sheet of your roll of toilet paper.
- Send an I-love-you note by registered mail to your loved one's office.
- Use a bar of soap to write "I love you" backwards on the rear windshield so that the words will read forward in the rearview mirror.
- Put notes in any items your loved one will open that day, such as a briefcase, purse or wallet, golf bag, schoolbook, or lunch box.
- Find an old pillowcase and write on it so that your loved one can end the day with a final "I love you."

- Some of Your Own Ideas:

_____

_____

_____

_____

_____

_____

_____

_____

_____

_____

_____

_____

_____

_____

_____

25 ♥ A Little TLC

Treat your loved one kind
Buy her a corsage
Have his shoes all shined
And give them a massage

The Idea: Treat the one you love to some tender, loving care. Do this because you want your loved one to have a fun day taking care of him or herself for a change, instead of caring for everyone else.

Setting a Budget: At first glance this may seem like an expensive idea, but it doesn't have to be that way. You can go all out and buy him or her everything listed below, or you can accomplish a similar goal by doing only one or two of the ideas suggested. Maybe you and your loved one have a mutual friend who would help you do some of the suggestions listed below for free or for a minimal amount, just to share in making the day special for the one you love.

Planning to Pamper: You can do many things for the one you love to make this day of pampering an unforgettable experience. Here are just a few activities you can schedule for him or her.

- A haircut or time with a hairdresser
- A manicure

- A massage by a masseuse
- Time at the department store to buy a new dress or suit
- An hour in a hot tub
- A sauna
- A nap

An Alternative: Instead of (or in addition to) treating the one you love to the above pampering, make some changes in your own appearance. If you're walking around with tangled hair, a stringy goatee, or holes in your jeans, try having your own hair styled, your face shaved, or buying yourself a new pair of slacks. If your nails are chipped and you haven't worn a dress in more than a year, get a manicure and put on something that makes you look and feel pretty. Your loved one just might fall in love with you all over again!

26 ♥ Theme Dates

Pick a theme, then send a card
Plan three new dates or four
It helps to keep them off their guard
When surprises are in store

The Idea: This way to say "I love you" is great if you are planning a surprise for the one you love, and you want to catch him or her off guard.

Plan a series of three or four dates centered around a theme. (Some suggested themes are listed below.) If you have an event planned that you don't want the one you love to suspect, such as a surprise party, you can incorporate it into date number three or four of your series.

Planning Theme Dates: Let's say a guy named Doug sends his girlfriend Cindy a card inviting her to go on a series of dates the first Saturday of each month over a period of four months. The dates will be centered around the theme of transportation.

August date: Doug and Cindy board a train and travel two hours to a quaint town where they enjoy a walk in the country and a romantic dinner at sunset. At the end of the day, they board the train and return to their hometown.

September date: While the weather is still warm, the

two journey to a nearby river where a paddle boat takes people for afternoon trips and then back to their original port for a riverside barbecue.

October date: To view the brilliant colors of changing fall leaves in nearby mountains, Doug and Cindy drive to a local aerial tramway that goes up the side of a mountain. At the top the two find an open meadow and eat a picnic lunch.

November date: Bundled in their wool sweaters to keep warm, Doug surprises Cindy by driving his car up to an awaiting hot air balloon. The huge aircraft, now aloft, is silhouetted against the orange sunset. Cindy is caught completely off guard when Doug opens a small black velvet box, removes a ring, places it on Cindy's finger, and says, "Cindy, I love you. Will you marry me?"

Had Doug not already planned a series of fun dates prior to the hot air balloon ride, Cindy might have been a little suspicious. Coming at the end of a series of dates with a similar theme, he was able to surprise his loved one with a very special gift.

Considering Other Themes:

- *North, South, East, and West—Plan a series of short journeys to nearby spots in each direction.*
- *The Four Seasons—Regardless of the time of year, choose a spring, summer, fall, and winter event.*
- *High and Low—Within a hundred miles of your home, find the highest elevation, the lowest elevation, and two locations in-between. Plan activities as close to these sites as possible.*
- *Aquatics—Visit a lake, a stream, an ocean, and a waterfall.*

27 ♥ One Day at a Time

How do I love thee?
Let me count the ways
From deep down inside me
Some thoughts for all your days

The Idea: You may have seen popular calendars showing "a joke a day," "a proverb a day," or "a quote a day." Here's your chance to create the same kind of calendar for the one you love.

This project can be as simple as providing love thoughts for a week, or, if you want to take the time, you can make enough pages for a month. If you really want to impress your loved one, create a calendar with 365 pages! We recommend the month-long option.

Preparing Your Love-Thought-for-the-Day Gift: Begin by purchasing either a nice calendar or a bound journal with blank pages. These items should be available in most stationery stores.

If you are preparing enough pages in a small journal for one month, number each two-page layout with the days of the month (1st, 2nd, 3rd, and so on). Don't bother putting in the names of the days of the week. Your loved one may want to use this calendar again in future months.

Now, write a brief thought on each page about why you love this special person, or tell what you like best about him or her.

Getting Your Mind (Heart) in Gear— Some Examples:

- 9th. Your sense of humor is unmatched by anyone. You make me laugh as no one else can.

- 14th. I love how you encourage me when I'm down.

- 25th. It's this simple. I love you.

- 30th. Thanks for spending so much time with me.

Presenting Your Love-Thought-for-the-Day Calendar: Once your journal is completed, buy a card that suits the moment and give it to the one you love at dinner. Explain that he or she can only look at each page on the day indicated. No fair looking ahead.

28 ❤ Pick a Project

Pick a project you want done
One you hoped they'd do
It can't be one that seems like fun
Or by now they'd be through!

The Idea: What better way to tell someone of your love than to perform some awful or tedious task that has been hanging over him or her like a gray cloud. It may be a project that the one you love has wanted done for a long time.

For example, you can pull all those weeds that ruin the view from your loved one's window. You can replace or wash all the screens on the doors. You can clean out the garage or that hall closet that hasn't been touched since you moved into the house.

Below we have provided a worksheet to help you plan your project. You might want to do this on a day when the one you love isn't home. Then the completed project can be your surprise gift.

Special Project Worksheet

Step One—Pick a Project

List below all the projects he or she would like to have done but doesn't want to do.

_____

_____

_____

_____

Now circle the least pleasant one. That's what you're going to do first.

Step Two—List Your Supplies

List the paints, tools, do-it-yourself books, and other items you may need.

_____   _____

_____   _____

_____   _____

_____   _____

Step Three—Get to Work!

Ending the Day: Once you have finished your project, show the one you love all the work you have done. Explain that you did the task because you loved him or her so much you wanted to take away a burden.

29 ❤ Row, Row, Row Your Boat

Drop all those pencils
Forget the chores
Stow your utensils
And trade them for oars

The Idea: Find a lake resort within driving distance where a rowboat can be rented. Don't even think of renting a boat with an outboard motor. We're talking about love, not noise.

Making Your Day Special: Before you leave for your aquatic excursion, here are some suggestions to consider as you plan your special day.

1. *You might want to pack an ice chest.* Bring your loved one's favorite snacks and beverages to enjoy on the lake. Bring along some old bread or crackers to feed the ducks too. Just in case the seats are not comfortable (which goes almost without saying in rowboats), take along a couple of cushions.

2. *Pick your loved one's favorite time of day.* If he or she is a morning person, go as early in the day as possible, while the water is still and the sounds are distinct. If the one you love enjoys the outdoors, go at midday to bask in the sunshine. Then, there's late afternoon. Fewer people are around, and the sun is

low in the sky. Your loved one may enjoy a boat ride just before sunset.

3. *Find a spot that is away from the crowd.* Don't row your entire time together. Bring in the oars and enjoy the time with the one you love. The only sounds you should hear are the lapping of the water on the side of your rowboat, the movement of nearby ducks, and your conversation.

4. *Tell him or her how great it is to be together.* Then say, "I love you."

30 ♥ Habit Reforming

*Quit a bad habit for those in your
   life
Take all that booze off the shelf
Give up on smoking just for your
   wife
Or give it all up for yourself*

The Idea: This idea revolves around telling at least two people that you love them—your most significant loved one and yourself. Do you have a habit or mannerism that irritates those around you? Maybe it's something as serious as eating too much, or maybe it's as minor as snapping your chewing gum. In any case, bad habits may be adding stress to your relationships with those you love.

You can show those close to you how much you care about them by changing those idiosyncrasies or bad habits that bother them.

Giving Up For Love: Here are a few examples of habits many of us could consider ending.

- Tapping a pen on the table
- Leaving the seat up on the toilet
- Cussing
- Leaving lights on in the house
- Chewing with your mouth open
- Returning the car without fuel

Breaking the Habit: Some habits are tough to break. Others may be more simple than you think. No matter how bad your habit, there is hope for change. Others have changed. You can do it too!

If the habit that annoys the one you love is basically harmless, ask him or her to tell you nicely when you are doing it. You may not even know you are doing it. Then take action to change your behavior. Here are some suggestions:

- If your habit is snapping your chewing gum, practice chewing with your mouth shut. Or, don't chew gum when you are around the one who gets annoyed.
- If your habit is whistling the same song over and over again, try humming softly instead.
- If your habit is picking your teeth, carry a toothbrush around.

If the habit you want to change is more serious, seek the help you need. For example, there are a number of programs designed to help you stop smoking. There are also programs to help you overcome addictions to drugs, alcohol, or other chemicals. We both work for a place that can help you overcome tough problems or addictions. Call us at 800-227-LIFE for help.

31 ♥ A Way When Away

Absence makes the heart grow fonder
You may know it's true
So when they travel far and yonder
Make them fonder too

The Idea: There almost always comes a time in the lives of people who love one another when they are separated. Husbands and wives are sometimes separated due to business trips, family events, or even retreat time spent alone. Parents are often separated from their children for any number of reasons, including summer camp, visits to grandparents, and going off to college.

Once we reach adulthood, many of us live thousands of miles from loved ones and family. This way to say "I love you" keeps us in touch with the people we love, whether it's a two-day trip or a year away from them. Here are some suggestions. You can use as few or as many as you like.

Leaving Love: *When the one you love is going away*

- Put a little gift in his or her luggage.
- Prepare a care package with candy, mints, gum, a book, or of things to do on an airplane, bus, or train.
- If your loved one is going away for more than two or three days, prepare a set of en-

velopes—one for each day he or she is gone. Put in each envelope a note, a photo of the two of you, and anything else that makes the one you love think of you.

When you are the one going away

- Call your loved one every day. Call more often if your budget permits.
- Leave a gift somewhere that will be found after you're gone.
- Make a cassette tape for the one you love to listen to while you're away.
- Call the ones you love and tell them you are going to watch a certain movie. Ask them to watch the same movie. Later you can talk about the movie as though you saw it together.

When the ones you love live far away

- Start calling them more often. If you usually call once a month, begin calling every other weekend. If you call once a week, begin calling twice a week.
- Drop a card telling them you miss them and love them. Assure your loved ones that you are doing well just knowing that they love you too.
- Instead of writing letters, record a cassette tape for them, telling them all about your

life. Not only is this easier than writing a note, they would probably love to hear your voice. Then ask them to send a tape back to you.

32 ♥ Once Upon a Time . . .

Before you say you cannot write
Let your mind go wild
Say "He's been my shining knight"
Or "She cooks like Julia Child"

The Idea: Most of us remember sitting down as little kids while an adult read from a book of fairy tales. Perhaps we most wanted to be like Cinderella, swept away from our dusty corner in the house to the fanciest ball in town. Or like Gulliver, we sought travel to faraway lands, visiting people much different from ourselves.

Now you can create a story of your own based on your relationship with the one you love. This idea is also appropriate for your entire family or any other group of friends or loved ones. Include as many people as you want in your story.

Preparing the Story: All you need is a pen, a pad of paper, and lots of imagination. You might try following these steps as well.

> 1. Go to your local library and wander through the children's books section. Sit down and read a few stories. Start with Dr. Seuss or stories by the Brothers Grimm.

2. Now, on separate pieces of paper, write down your name and the name of each loved one you want included in the story. Start listing the positive attributes about each person and some fun facts about their background.

3. Write your story by telling about your childhood and the childhood of the one you love. Talk about how you met. Explain your present situation. Let your mind go wild about the future. You might even use the ending: ". . . and they lived happily ever after."

A Sample Fairy Tale: Now, let's look at a fairy tale about a flight attendant from Tucson who met her Floridian contractor husband while they were in college at Notre Dame. (The story is written as if a husband wrote it for his wife.)

Once upon a time there was a cute little princess named Cathy who lived in the desert. Her long blonde hair was shiny and soft. Her eyes were as blue as the sky. She and her two sisters often walked through the desert picking wildflowers.

Far away, in another land near a great ocean, a little prince ran with his new puppy along the shoreline. An only child, Billy hoped one day to find a very special friend.

Cathy grew to be a pretty young woman and went to a land called Indiana to further her education. Meanwhile, Billy decided to attend college in the same land. One day when the air outside was crisp and snow was falling, Billy saw Cathy warming her hands near the fire in the student lounge. She was so pretty, in her soft pink sweater and winter coat. He had never seen anyone so beautiful before. He knew then that she was the special friend he had always wanted.

Cathy and Billy became friends, married, and flew away on a cloud. He builds gingerbread houses in meadows. She sails high above the Earth on the wings of a big silver cagle.

Every morning when Prince Billy awakens, he gazes at his princess and thanks God for his special gift. As they journey into the future, they gaze ahead at the hillsides covered with blue and red flowers. Above the rolling hills before them are the words "Billy Loves Cathy" written in the sky.

The Big Day: Once your story is completed and you feel good about it, set a date with the one you love. Find a location that has some relationship to your story, the flowered hillside, the desert plain. Take him or her there. Sit down together and read the story.

Going a Step Further: If you really want to impress the one you love, here are some ideas to make your fairy tale even more fun.

- Have someone you know do illustrations for the story.
- Wear a goofy costume that will add some humor.
- Bring objects mentioned in your story.
- Have your story printed and bound to make a memento the one you love will always cherish.

33 ❤ Adoption Papers

Give a gift or plant a tree
Adopt for them a bear
You can help the Earth you see
And tell loved ones you care

The Idea: You can tell someone you love him or her by doing good deeds. If the one you love has a special interest in some cause, has actively volunteered for a charity, or has spent time trying to save a part of our Earth, show him or her that you support that interest.

Saying "I Love You" by Giving to Others or Adopting a Cause: There are a variety of ways you can help the Earth, your city, the local environment, or unfortunate people while at the same time telling someone, "I love you."

> *Plant a tree.* Find a place in your city where you can plant a tree in the name of the one you love. Many cities allow this in community parks or along public roads. (You could even plant a tree for each member of your family.) Then, occasionally, you can go by to see how much the tree has grown. If you can't find a public place to plant a tree, do it in your own backyard.

> *Adopt an animal.* Most city zoos today have a

program where you can adopt one of their animals by making a donation or by becoming a "friend of the zoo." If the one you love loves animals, this might be an appropriate thing to do.

Donate to charity. If the one you love is active in some charity, make a special contribution to that charity in his or her name. You might even be able to take up a collection from friends and tell your loved one that the total donation will be dedicated to that special work.

Adopt a highway. Some cities, counties, or states allow you to adopt a segment of a highway. If there is no such program near you, you can get one started and designate the one you love as the adopter. You can visit that stretch of highway, and do your part to make sure it is free of litter.

Contribute to a building project. Often community theaters, churches, university buildings, and other public-oriented buildings under construction are projects that need people to donate in various amounts. You may be able to donate enough to dedicate a seat in the local community playhouse in the name of the one you love.

34 ❤ True Blue

No better way to show you care
Than when they're down and out
Find some time of yours to share
That's what love's all about

The Idea: Everyone has had a bad day. Some of us have even had bad weeks! There is no time in a person's life when he or she needs to feel loved more than when the gray clouds appear. Usually there are reasons why we become depressed.

- Someone close to us has moved away, and we miss this special person.
- We just had a rotten day at work.
- A loved one is ill.
- We just feel lonely.

Sometimes we can't explain what's wrong. We just have the blues.

Taking Away the Blues: Some people try to make their loved ones laugh their pain away. If that works for the one you love, give it a try. The laughter you create may be just the sunshine needed to break through some of the clouds. But if you are not able to humor the one you love out of the blues, try some of these simple ideas.

Just sit with them. Many of us are so uncomfortable when someone is depressed that we flee. We may feel like we must keep talking to lessen our own anxiety, or we may feel compelled to offer solutions that we know won't work. But someone who really feels blue usually doesn't want to hear half-baked solutions. That person just needs us to be there. Don't try to "fix" anything. Just be there.

Listen. If you sit with the person long enough, he or she may be able to talk to you. Often, a person with the blues just needs someone to hear his or her woes. Even if the situation doesn't sound so bad to you, it's certainly important to the person who's depressed. Be nearby and ready to listen.

Affirm your love. The best help we can sometimes give a friend or loved one who is hurting is the affirmation that he or she is worth our love. Let the person know you care. Let him or her know you will be there to help.

Hug them. There are people around you every day who may not have received a hug for months. If there's a person in your life who is hurting, try giving him or her a hug.

35 ❤ This Is Your Life

*Send them back and make them
    sob
With those who meant the most
Monty Hall will need a job
For you're a game show host*

The Idea: Anyone born before 1960 should remember the television show in which Ralph Edwards would surprise and honor someone on stage. Various people who had been a part of the honored person's life would appear from behind a curtain and share a personal story. You can provide the same kind of adventure for the one you love. (Here's your chance to find out what Pammy Sue, his old high school sweetheart, is really like. Track her down and invite her—if you dare.)

It is probably best to keep this idea a surprise. If your loved one knows in advance that you are planning a "This-Is-Your-Life" event, much of the excitement will be taken away. Granted, this idea is a little more time-consuming than some others in this book, but you can do a simplified version and have just as much fun.

Preparing for the Big Night: Although you could hold this event during the day, it might be more appropriate in the evening. Most of your preparation for this particular idea will take place prior to the Big Night. This event will be least expensive and most successful if you apply it to a loved one who is living close to where his or her roots are. Or, if you and the one you love are planning a trip to your loved one's hometown, perhaps you can plan ahead and have this event happen while he or she is "home."

- First, clear a date about two months in advance with the one you love. You're going to need some time to implement your plan.

- Go through your loved one's old pictures, scrapbooks, or other nostalgic items. As you find people who have been influential in your loved one's life, write down their names. You might also ask your loved one's family members if they have any names to suggest or if they think the names you have are good ones. If you are applying this idea to someone you grew up with, this step should be quite easy for you.

- Track down as many of the people on your list as you can. Ask them if they are available and if they would be willing to be a part of this special evening.

- Begin preparing your script. Find out a tidbit of relevant information that was unique to each person's relationship with the one you love. Think of something appropriate to say and something appropriate for each person to say before appearing "on stage."

- Select a location. You may want to invite all of your loved one's friends. Or you may want to make this an intimate event with only close family and friends. Whatever you decide, pick your location accordingly. It can be as simple as a friend's home or as elaborate as a banquet room at a nearby hotel.

Staging the Big Night: You should make sure that all the surprise guests arrive well before the scheduled arrival of the one you love. Put them in a room located behind the place where the guest of honor will sit. When the guest of honor appears, have everyone in the "audience" say, THIS IS YOUR LIFE! Once the one you love has gotten over the shock and embarrassment of such a greeting, tell him or her not to turn around at any time. Then, bring on your first guest.

Making the Night More Memorable: Here are a few items that can make the special night a living memory that will last forever.

- In keeping with the original "This Is Your Life" program, make up a scrapbook for the evening. A photo of each surprise guest could be featured. A handwritten message expressing personal sentiments can be placed next to each photo.

- Have a banner hanging above the chair where the guest of honor will be seated.
- After the last surprise guest is introduced, allow your loved one to say a few words.

36 ♥ Roast the Turkey

Gather friends who mean the most
Tell them to prepare
For a very special roast
But do it all with care

The Idea: You have probably seen a celebrity on television "roasted" by his or her peers. A roast is an event where one person is honored through a series of presentations or speeches by his or her friends, family, coworkers, or others. Each speaker takes a turn poking fun at the personality traits or life experiences of the honoree. Usually, a roast occurs as part of an evening dinner party.

We suggest you do the same for the one you love. You don't need to rent a banquet room at the local hotel. Keep it simple. Hold a dinner at your home and invite some of your closest friends.

Comedian Don Rickles used to be the king of roasts. His jokes and barbs were quite direct. However, we suggest you use sensitivity when implementing this idea for the one you love. Remember, the intention is to have the guest of honor laughing *with* the audience.

Selecting Your Presenters: At least a week before your roast, make a list of all those people you think should be presenters. Select a good cross section of the people who are part of your loved one's life. For example, pick one or two coworkers, a couple of clever family members, someone from church, a neighbor, and an old high school friend.

Providing Suggestions for the Presenters: You might want to give each presenter an assigned topic based on their relationship to the one you love. For example, Nick, a successful yet compulsive executive, might be roasted by the following people.

> *His boss* may be asked to "roast" his behavior at work: Nick is a "detail man." He would know if someone had been sitting at his desk by checking to see if one of the ten pencils in his drawer had been used without being resharpened.
>
> *His golfing buddy* may be asked about his golf game: Nick is the only guy I know that walks off the golf course with more golf balls than he brought. He spends more time collecting balls others have lost than he does playing the game. Nick, have you ever purchased a golf ball in your life?
>
> *A fellow elder at church* may be asked to explain Nick's behavior in a board meeting: We can always rely on Nick to make sure the minutes of the last meeting are correct. Not only does he take his own notes to keep track of each detail, he corrects the spelling and grammar of everything that's passed out.

Affirming the Roastee: Since you are trying to show the one you love how much he or she is
loved, be sure each speaker ends with some words of
affirmation and encouragement. It's fun to laugh at
our own idiosyncrasies, but it's better yet to receive
praise for our quirks and foibles that are endearing
to others.

37 ♥ Money Is No Object

Go off on a shopping spree
Bring along your honey
Get the best gift there could be
'Cause you will spend no money

The Idea: One way to say "I love you" is to go on a shopping spree and buy the one you love as many gifts as possible. But since most people don't have enough money to do that, this suggestion is a little different. You're still going on a shopping spree with the one you love—you just aren't going to spend any money.

Outlining Your Day: Your goal for the day is to explore a series of shops together. Once you are in a store, go your separate ways, each of you searching for the perfect gift for the other (regardless of the cost).

Then, when you have rejoined one another, show your loved one the gift you have selected. Let your loved one show you the gift he or she selected for you. Put both of the items back and leave the store. This kind of shopping doesn't cost you a dime, and you'll have loads of fun finding the perfect gift. Here are a couple of examples of how to shop when "money is no object."

The card shop. Search high and low for the card that describes your feelings for the one you love. Once you've found the card, show it to him or her. Let your loved one read it, and then put it back. If you had fun finding the first card, you may want to search for several more.

The department store. You can do this kind of shopping one department at a time. Find the perfect suit, shirt, tie, and shoes for him. Find the right dress, scarf, accessories, and pumps for her. Then go to the jewelry department and then perfumes. Share your discoveries with the one you love.

You might also go into a pet store and find the pet you'd most like to give the one you love. Or go into a furniture store and select the piece of furniture you'd most like to give him or her.

(A hint to make sure you really follow the rules: Leave the cash, credit cards, and checkbook at home!)

Making the Most of This Idea: The primary benefit of this idea is that you and the one you love will be spending another fun-filled afternoon or evening together. Plus, you may find out some great ideas for upcoming birthday or Christmas gifts. So take along your notepad. It might come in handy.

38 ❤ Book Ends

Get a book, their favorite one
You can leather bind it
But do some more, for you're not
done
Until the author's signed it

The Idea: Perhaps one of the people in your life loves to read. Even if the one closest to you doesn't read much, he or she probably has a favorite book. Here's your chance to give a special surprise, just to say "I love you."

Making Their Favorite Book a Special Gift: Below we have provided several suggestions of how you can use something as simple as a favorite book and make it a special and treasured gift.

> *First Edition.* If your loved one's favorite book is old, search used bookstores in your area on the chance that they may have a first or second printing copy. If you can't find a copy locally, ask a bookstore manager who carries rare books if he or she can direct you to a service that helps people find out-of-print and first edition books.
>
> *Leather Bound.* Even if you can't find an original issue of the favorite book, you can take a more recently published copy and have it pro-

fessionally bound in a nice-looking, long-lasting leather cover.

Personalized. Write a very special and personal message on the inside cover of the book. Be sure to say "I love you" somewhere in that message.

Autographed. If the author of the book is still living, do whatever you can to have him or her sign your first edition or leather-bound copy of the book. You may want to send the book to them via certified mail, providing a shipping box and enough postage to return it to you. (Just in case this book becomes the favorite book of the one you love, we have autographed it for you below.)

39 ♥ Auto Mate

Some day before they leave in the morn
Do crazy things to their car
Make other drivers lean on their horn
And tell them how in love you are

The Idea: Before the one you love leaves for work one morning, decorate the car as someone might decorate a wedding car. This will be your special way of declaring your love publicly.

Preparing the Car: Below we have given just a few examples of what you can do to your loved one's car to let him or her—and the world—know of your love.

- *Place signs on the car.* Say things like "Mike loves Debra" or "Annie loves Allen." Put one on the back of the car that says "Linda loves Vince. Honk if you love someone today too!"
- *Put things inside the car.* Try filling every square inch of the backseat with colorful balloons.
- *Put a cassette tape in the car.* Record a message telling your loved one how much you love him or her.
- *Give your loved one some treats.* Put his or

her favorite candy, cookie, or munchie in the seat.

- *Write him or her a note.* Tell your loved one that you will clean up the car when he or she gets home.

40 ♥ Top 40

*Choose some songs, your favorite
    hits
From "Sunny" to "Stormy
    Weather"
Act as DJ, use your wits
Then put it all together*

The Idea: Music is one way people have been saying "I love you" for centuries. If you're a sentimentalist at all, you should know some songs that really set the mood for love. If you don't know who your loved one's favorite singer or musician is, find out.

Making Musical Memories: Here are a few suggestions of how you can use music with your loved ones. Some are very simple; others may take some time to prepare.

> *Make a tape.* If you and the one you love have known each other for a few years, you probably know some songs that bring special meaning to your relationship. Gather these songs together and record them on one tape using a home stereo system. You may want to add a narrative before each song, describing the setting where you first heard it. This idea would be especially appropriate for two old friends getting together after many years. For example, if you graduated from high school in 1968, gather some songs from that year. Play the

tape while you are together just to make your day even more nostalgic. (If you do not have the equipment or songs to make a tape on your own, many major record stores can make a custom tape for you incorporating almost any song you choose.)

Attend a musical play or movie together. Find a local community theater or a major performing arts center near you and attend a musical —especially if it is a love story. May we recommend an old Rodgers and Hammerstein musical such as "Carousel" or "The Sound of Music"? Buy the soundtrack in advance, and you can listen to the love songs on your way home.

Write a love song. While this idea is not appropriate for everyone, there are people who can write music for those they love. If you have no musical talent, rewrite the lyrics of a song specifically for the one you love. To make it fun, take a tune such as the theme song from an old television show like "Gilligan's Island," and substitute a story about yourself and the one you love.

Go to a concert. Find out your loved one's favorite musical performer. Even if you like rock and roll and his favorite singer is a country western star, go ahead and get the tickets. You might just enjoy yourself too.

Buy a tape. If there are no concerts near your city, or if her favorite performer is not coming to town, buy her a tape, album, or disc of her favorite group.

If none of our suggestions appeal to you, just get in the car, turn on some music, and sing your favorite songs together.

41 ♥ A Thousand Words

Van Gogh was quite an artist
From sunflowers to oceans
Now you can try your hardest
To paint from your emotions

The Idea: They say a picture is worth a thousand words. Have you ever been with someone and analyzed some great piece of art? You might have looked closely at the artist's technique and tried to figure out what prompted him or her to create that particular work.

Psychologists do much the same thing with the drawings of little children. Often the setting and actions depicted by children can inform professionals of the innermost thoughts a child may have. As adults we can do the same expressive artwork we did as children in order to show the love we have for others.

Making Art Work: This idea involves an activity you and the one you love can do together. Using one of the ideas listed below, set aside two or three hours for the sole purpose of creating a piece of art for the one you love. Work in the same location but completely independent of one another.

After purchasing your art supplies, begin simply by saying something like this: "In the next two hours I am going to do my best to create a painting that expresses my love for you. I am asking you to do the same. It doesn't have to be attractive or make sense to anyone else. When we're done, we're going to explain why we painted what we did for one another."

Selecting a Happy Medium: There are virtually an unlimited variety of art materials you could use for this activity. Here are a few of the more simple suggestions you could implement.

> *Oil Painting*—Buy two medium-sized blank canvas boards, a set of oil paints, and a few brushes. Share the paints, but don't look at each other's work until it's finished.

> *Water Colors*—Perhaps the easiest medium to use is water colors. You can buy water colors relatively inexpensively. And unlike the oil painting, which requires a canvas, water colors can be done on art paper.

> *Finger Paints*—Regress to childhood and create your picture using colorful finger paints.

> *Pastels or Pencil Sketching*—Some people may find pastels or pencil drawings easier to do than any type of paint.

> *Clay*—Use some Play-Doh or other flexible clay to sculpt a series of objects that tell a story during your sharing time.

Crayons—There is nothing wrong with making this activity simple. Each of you can sit down with a box of crayons. That's how we told stories as little kids. Why not do it again!

Giving an Art Show: When you and the one you love have finished creating your works of art, show each other what you have created. Explain what it means to you. Then, prop up your creations. Sit back and start a thousand-word conversation. What do you see in your loved one's creation that he or she might not even realize is there? What further insights do you each have about your drawings, paintings, or other creations?

42 ♥ Extra! Extra!

Start the presses! Beat the dead-
lines!
No more morning blues
Let your loved one read the head-
lines
Now they're front page news!

The Idea: Imagine getting up in the morning and shuffling to the front door to get the morning paper. The brisk air chills your bones, you yawn as you close the door, and then you open the paper and see your name in headlines:

_____ **NAMED**

THE MOST LOVABLE PERSON IN TOWN!

As you read on, you find out that all the articles on the front page are love notes just for you. Your day has brightened. You seem to glide on air as you prepare your morning cup of coffee.

Acting as Editor and Publisher: You may not be able to print a newspaper front page that would look just like your local paper, but you can create a mock front page filled with articles about the one you love.

Before any newspaper can be printed, a publisher needs a team of talented writers and reporters. He or she also needs a means of printing the paper. In case you have no experience in such endeavors, here are some simple steps to follow in creating this "special edition."

1. Decide what topics should be covered in your newspaper. Perhaps you'll want to get out a copy of your local paper and thumb through the various sections to get some ideas.

Main news—Make this the article where you tell about this special-edition newspaper honoring the most lovable person in town.

Comics—Have a friend or family member write a funny story about your loved one's sense of humor. Get an illustrator, if you can.

Editorial—Have someone write a tongue-in-cheek opinion article answering a question like: "Why Everyone Should Be as Lovable as _____"

Sports section—Have a friend who golfs with your loved one write an article about his or her ever-improving golf game.

Life section—Honor the one you love by having someone do a feature article about his or her life.

2. Select a group of reporters and assign a deadline of about ten days from the date you give them the project. Ask each to write no more than one-and-a-half pages, double spaced. Your reporters can include family members and friends. For instance, if you do this for your husband on Father's Day, you could have your children write stories and draw pictures featuring Dad.

3. Once you have received your manuscripts from the various reporters (or once you are done writing the articles yourself if you are working alone), read through each article, making sure that they will be uplifting and fun for the one you love.

4. Now get creative. Write the headlines. The headline of a newspaper is the most important feature because it must draw attention to a story in just a few words.

5. After the articles have been written and edited, the headlines composed, and any photos or illustrations gathered, it's time to go to print. At one extreme, you can take your articles and headlines to a local typesetter and have them typeset in newspaper format, or you can have a local paste-up artist lay out your newspaper and make it ready for printing. Be sure to give bylines for those who contributed articles.

At the other extreme, you can get a blank sheet of newsprint-sized paper and hand print all of your articles. You can compromise somewhere between these two extremes by typing the articles on a standard typewriter and then pasting them to your paper. Of course, if you have access to desktop publishing equipment and software, you can produce a very professional-looking paper. Don't feel bad if you cannot have your paper typeset. Chances are the more simple and handmade the paper looks, the more it will be cherished.

6. Finally, it is time to distribute your paper. You may want to fold it inside a real newspaper to make sure the one you love sees it. Or you may simply want to hand over your front page and say, "Have you read the paper today?"

43 ❤ Movie Mania

Find a movie house near you
Pick a film that's right
See a matinee at two
Or drive-in late at night

The Idea: Take the one you love to a movie, but don't just go on Friday or Saturday night. Use one of the creative suggestions below to make the outing more fun, out of the ordinary, or romantic.

Getting Out of the Rut: Maybe you always go to the movies at the same theater. Maybe you go to the theater only on certain nights. Maybe you see the same kind of movie every time you go. Try adding a little variety to your life. Perhaps one of the ideas below will change your movie-going habits and create a new way of saying "I love you."

> *Go to a drive-in.* Going to a drive-in is something we all did as children but don't do very often as adults. There are many advantages to going to drive-ins, if you really think about it. You don't have to worry about how you look because the only people seeing you are the people going to the movie with you. A drive-in movie can also be more appropriate if you want to talk with each other during the movie. Still another advantage of the drive-in is the

fact that you can take lots of the people you love with you. Just borrow someone's van.

Go to a matinee. Some Saturday afternoon, drop everything, lock the doors, and find a movie you've wanted to see. If you live in a busy city where at night there are lines for the best movies, you can probably avoid the crowd by attending a matinee. When you leave the theater the sun will still be out! That will give you enough time in the day to find another way to say "I love you."

Rent a movie. If you have a VCR in your home, go to the video rental store and find a movie you both love. On the way home, buy some popcorn and your favorite beverage. Relax at home where you are most comfortable.

Go to an old movie. In some cities there are theaters that run old movies. If you have never seen some of the classics such as "Casablanca" or "Gone with the Wind" or "The Thirty-nine Steps," see one of these with the one you love.

Go to an old theater. Even though most of us are spoiled today with modern theater stereo systems, comfortable chairs, and air conditioning, there is something nostalgic about finding the oldest theater in your area and going to a movie there.

Have your own film festival. Select several film classics now on video and watch them during one evening or weekend with people who share your love of, say, the Marx brothers, W. C. Fields, or Marilyn Monroe. Your public library may have these films for loan.

44 ❤ Lights, Camera, Action

Though you do not work out at
Disney or Warner
Someday that may be correct
You may see your star on some
Hollywood corner
From making a film you'll direct

The Idea: Home movies have come a long way. Back in the sixties we'd have to wait weeks or months for Dad to use up the film, have it developed, rent a projector, and then find a wall large and white enough to double as a screen. And then, we'd see a scratchy film showing unrecognizable people.

Today you can use a home video camera, shoot an event, and then run into the house for all present to view *and* hear. Now you can show your loved one how much he or she is loved by secretly filming a movie starring all the loved ones in his or her life.

Obtaining Your Equipment: Although home video cameras are becoming a possession almost as common as microwave ovens, many people do not yet have one. If you don't have a friend who will lend a video camera to you, one can be rented from a camera store.

Preparing Your Production: Try to keep your video project fun, meaningful, and memorable for all involved. In each of the ideas listed below you have the option of preparing a detailed script or simply ad-libbing the whole show.

Have close friends be the "stars" of your production. Because your film is meant to be a surprise, have someone dress up as the one you love, and feature him or her as the leading man or woman.

Selecting Your Format: Here are some suggested formats for you to consider. You may have some ideas of your own.

> *"A Day in the Life of_____"*—Narration by the camera operator: "Meet _____. Here he is coming out of the front door of his lovely home. This is his wife. Together they have brought into the world four precious sons shown here playing flag football on the front lawn."

> *Create an evening news program*—Assemble a simplified set using a table and backdrop. Have each person in your cast serve as various newscasters. Report the latest news about your loved one's work, family, and friends.

> *Produce a series of television commercials*— This may be the easiest idea yet. Take a photo of your loved one and place it on the front of

an old mayonnaise jar. Have ten friends hold up the jar explaining why they would recommend your loved one to anyone. They might say, "He's the best friend I ever had." "He encourages me when I'm down." "He's the most helpful coworker in our office." "I would recommend this product to anyone who's looking for a friend."

45 ♥ A Friend in Need

When helping one who's lonely
Or someone who is blue
Bring your one and only
And they'll feel better too

The Idea: Somehow when we do things for other people out of an act of love, we receive even more love in return. Have you and the one you love ever spent some time with a hungry person? Have you ever visited a lonely person in prison? Why not multiply the love in your own hearts by sharing it with someone who may not feel loved at all?

Selecting the One in Need: Finding someone to serve should not be difficult. And there are hundreds of ways you could help a person who is hurting. We've listed a few ideas to get you started.

The homeless—There are thousands of homeless men, women, and children in America. Not all homeless people are mentally ill or alcoholics. Many are people like you or me who have fallen onto tough times. Call your local rescue mission or the International Union of Gospel Missions in Kansas City, Missouri, to see how you can help.

The lonely—Without even calling a service organization in town you may be able to think of a friend, someone at work, or a member of your church who would appreciate your company. Invite him or her over to dinner. Take him or her to the movies with you. Sit and listen to the person talk. Your presence can make the day seem brighter.

The prisoner—There are many organizations such as Prison Fellowship who are looking for people to visit and assist those serving time in prison. Find out what you can do to help.

The children—Consider sponsoring a child in a poor nation through organizations like World Vision. Together you and your loved one can write letters of encouragement and friendship to a little person you probably will never meet. Or, you can sign up to participate in a local Big Brothers/Big Sisters program and help a child in your own town.

46 ♥ Ad Vantage

Create yourself an ad campaign
Come on now, what the heck
You may do well and hired to train
An agency exec

The Idea: Write an ad campaign? You won't need to create ad copy that will be featured on Madison Avenue or create a famous jingle. Just use the various media that are around you on a daily basis to create an ad campaign implementing the theme, "[Carolyn] loves you."

Make your campaign last a day, a week, or an entire month. To keep it simple you may want to use one or two of the ideas suggested below throughout the year.

Advertising Your Love: Try these simple suggestions.

Method of advertising	*Your campaign*
Billboard	Stand on a street corner where you know the one you love will be driving by and hold up a large sign displaying your slogan, [ROB] LOVES [DINA]. Take it a step further and have several people do this on corners along your

loved one's route home from work. Make your own personalized [SALLY] LOVES [STEVE] bumper sticker.

Radio

If you can't create your own radio ad, call up a radio station and request a song for your loved one. Pick a special song and ask the DJ to say something like, "This song is dedicated to a very special couple in San Pedro. Rob wants to let you know how much he loves you, Dina."

Television

Cut out a piece of paper the size of your television screen. Write across it in large, bold letters, "I love you." You may want to paste a picture of the two of you on the paper too. Then attach it to the front of your television.

Direct mail

Direct mail advertising includes those letters you receive in the mail daily from unknown solicitors. Simply take an envelope and make it look like the personalized direct mail you receive. Inside,

	simply write the words: I love [Tom].
Magazine ads	Get her a copy of her favorite magazine. Over one of the existing full-page advertisements, paste a sheet of paper that simply has the I-love-you words from your campaign.
Newspaper ads	Buy space in a local newspaper and run your own ad telling the one you love how much you care for him or her.

Perhaps you can think of more ideas as you are bombarded daily with advertisements. You can alter the above ideas to honor a son or daughter or to congratulate a colleague for a job well done.

47 ♥ An Advent Sure

During the month of December
Create some more joy each day
Make it a month to remember
With a calendar done in your way

The Idea: Some of the best activities from childhood are forgotten in adulthood, like having an Advent calendar at Christmas. Most of us probably don't get such a calendar any more unless there are children in the house. This idea allows you to create a special calendar for the one you love.

Creating Your I-Love-You Calendar: Since we want to keep this project as simple as possible, we suggest you start with a store-bought Advent calendar. You can buy one for next to nothing right after Christmas.

Most of these calendars are created by gluing two sheets of paper together. The front page of heavier paper contains the windows that are opened. The thinner paper on the back has the pictures placed to show through the windows.

Carefully remove that back page. Then, in each location where a drawing is found, place a special message or photo that will bring joy to the one you love as he or she opens each window throughout the month. If you cannot remove the back sheet, open each window and paste your object over the existing picture. Close the windows and seal them with a small piece of tape or a small adhesive dot.

Selecting Items for Your Windows:
Here are a few ideas for the windows of your calendar.

- Photos of you and the one you love
- Photos of children or mutual friends
- Directions that might say, "Look under your bed" (hide a gift in that location)
- One- or two-word messages that are meaningful for the two of you

48 ♥ Camera Sly

Using photos from your past
And captions you have written
Give a memory that will last
When older you'll be gettin'

The Idea: There are many ways you can use photos to say "I love you." Grandchildren give them to grandparents all the time. We take pictures when we graduate from high school, when we get married, and when the first child is born. Why not use celluloid sentimentality to your best advantage? Here are some ideas:

Create a scrapbook of your times together. Trace your relationship with your loved one back to the time it began. If you have loved this person for any length of time, you probably have collected some pictures over the months or years. Take those pictures, put them in a scrapbook, and write your own captions for each. Make some comments sentimental and others humorous. Present the scrapbook to your loved one and go through it together.

Create a scrapbook of your childhood or your loved one's. Find either your baby pictures or your loved one's and make a scrapbook. Make up captions like, "Here you are wearing your mother's high-heeled shoes at the age of nine. You looked pretty then and you look pretty now!" Or, "Jeff at twelve. He was so tall, the coach asked him to put new nets on the basketball hoops. Nice legs!"

Make a poster. Take one of your favorite pictures of the two of you; have it blown up into a poster with a message like "Scott loves Jenny."

Have a portrait taken. If your budget will handle the expense, go out and have a nice portrait made of you and the one you love. Or, give him or her a certificate to have a portrait taken alone.

Frame your favorites. If the one you love has some favorite photos of you and the others he or she loves, have some of them framed and give them as a surprise gift.

Send them off. If you have parents, children, grandparents, or other loved ones who live in various parts of the country or world, send them pictures of you and those in your life regularly. Make them feel that they are a part of the activities and changes in your life.

49 ♥ Fa La La La La La La La La

Chestnuts roasting on an open fire
Shop before the stores all close
Yuletide carols sung with those you
*   admire*
And gifts wrapped up in pretty
*   bows*

The Idea: Ah, Christmas time. What better season of the year to say "I love you." Aside from the obvious traditional method of giving gifts, we suggest some other activities to make your next Christmas one that is filled with love for those special people in your life.

Here are some ways to say "I love you" to those in your family or to others who are especially close.

- Promise to do most of the Christmas shopping this coming year.
- Volunteer to wrap all the gifts.
- Take them out to look at the city's Christmas lights.
- Cook the Christmas dinner.
- Spend a little more money on them this year, if you can afford it.
- Invite close friends over to sing Christmas carols.

- Spend a night at home roasting chestnuts or popping corn in the fireplace.
- Build a snowman together.
- If you're far from home, surprise loved ones with a visit.

Sharing with Some Other Family: This Christmas the love within your own family can be multiplied many times over if you make it a special year for some less fortunate family. Call your local social services office or a church to find out the name of a family needing help. Here are some ideas of what you can do for them:

- Find out the ages of the children and buy each an appropriate gift.
- Surprise them one evening with a Christmas tree and ornaments.
- Invite them to join your family for Christmas dinner.
- The most appropriate actions might best be done anonymously, like donating a turkey for the family's Christmas dinner.

50 ♥ Just Say It!

You have seen so many new ways
Yet you know that you're never
*   through*
So practice a lot throughout all your
*   days*
By saying the words, "I love you"

The Idea: We can't state it much more simply than the title of this suggestion. Just say it! We've shown you some clever ways to spend time with the ones you love, to express your feelings for them, and to have a lot of fun in the process. Throughout every day, we all could use another affirmation that we are loved.

Here are some simple, everyday activities you can do to encourage and remind those around you that they are loved.

- Give simple, inexpensive gifts on unexpected days.
- Dance with your loved one in your living room.
- Tell the people you love you are grateful for their friendship.
- Send them a FAX that says "I love you."
- Pray with them.
- Say "I'm sorry," "I was wrong," or "Please forgive me" when it needs to be said.
- Send a greeting card for no specific reason.
- Greet them with a smile and a hug every day.

- Write a special someone a love letter.
- Buy them a pet.
- Hold them when they cry.
- Stay home with your loved one an extra night in the week.
- Learn how to say "I love you" in sign language.
- Walk up, put your arms around someone you love, and say, "I love you."

II. ♥ Ways to Tell Your Child "I Love You"

Dedicated to

Johanna
Mary
Kurt, Katelyn, Kiersten
and to all the
children who know me as
"Aunt Jan"

✦ Contents

✦ Introduction

As common as the phrase "I love" is in our culture, love is not *always* an easy thing to feel. Why? Because loving people requires setting self aside momentarily and focusing our devotion, attention, and affection upon someone other than ourselves. Love is, above all things, unselfish. And most of us are more self-centered than we care to admit.

Still, it is relatively easy to *feel* love compared to how difficult it is for many people to *express* their love. We often find it easier to declare that we "love" a new broccoli recipe or a pair of shoes than to state openly that we love a certain person.

Why is it often difficult for us to express our love? Because love is rooted in giving, and giving is most fulfilling if that which one gives is received. The possibility that someone might not receive what we desire to give makes us vulnerable. Vulnerability carries with it the possibility of rejection, and, in that, embarrassment and an emotional sting. Thus, the greatest, most exhilarating and uplifting emotion we can know also carries within it the potential for the greatest emotional pain. For many people, love goes unexpressed because love carries this risk. These people rarely know great moments of joy, because they fear the possibility of pain.

For others, love goes unstated because the person simply doesn't know how to express the love he or she feels. Perhaps she hasn't been trained in giving or has never been shown love and, therefore, doesn't know how to show it. Perhaps he doesn't know from experience what is most likely to be received and valued as an expression of love. That is where this book can help.

Here are ways to show love, to express love in the language that children understand. You will learn to tell your child how you feel with minimal risk and maximal joy.

Many other ways are possible, of course. Let this be just the beginning of your telling your child, "I love *you!*" The good news is that there is no more rewarding enterprise on the face of the earth than to love and be loved by a child.

1 ✦ Make a Pledge to Love Your Child

Make *your* love your child's number-one birthright. Count it as the most valuable gift you will ever give your child—greater than your home, greater than any material possessions you might provide, even greater than anything you can teach or show to your child. Your child needs to know that he has your love as an absolute, a given, a known entity in his life.

Let your child know your love is something he can always count on. Admit to your child that there may be times when you don't say you love him—in fact, there may be moments when your child does not even think it to be true—but that, nonetheless, your love is constant.

Vows of Love *"Kiddo, I may not have told you lately, but guess what? It's still true."*

"What's true?"

"The number-one, all-encompassing, never-to-be-denied, absolutely positive fact that I love you."

Let your child know that your love is not rooted in anything she does, but that you love her simply because she is your child.

"Honey, I will love you forever."

"Son, I will love you always."

"Daughter, I love you more than all the universe and everything in it."

Let your child know that your love for him is a divine gift from God to you for him.

"God must have loved us a great deal to have blessed us with a son like you."

"I just can't help it. God put a great big dose of love in my heart for you, daughter. Nothing can change that. God put it there, and He has assured me that I'm going to have this love for you forever."

What if you don't feel this spontaneous love for your child? Make that your problem, not your child's. Get help. Seek counsel. Question why you don't love. Face the fact that the problem is within you, not resident in your child. And determine that you *will* love your child. You will get the help you need, you will make loving your child your number-one priority as a parent.

Make a vow of your love. It may be at a reception after the christening, baptism, or dedication of your child. It may be in the form of a toast at a family dinner. Don't just feel your pledge of love—declare it. Confess it to others. Speak it. Put it into words. Make it a declaration in time and space. Ask other family members to support you in your pledge to love your child. Don't keep your vow a secret from your child. Let your child know that you have made a pledge to love him always.

Certificates of Love One way to express your love for your child is to declare your child's birthright of love with a "Love Certificate" of some type. One couple added this line to their child's birth certificate: "Conceived in love, birthed with love, and with God's help, nurtured to adulthood by love."

Another couple wrote out a "Parents' Pledge" to their children. They worked on the statement together during the pregnancy of their first child, had a calligrapher write it out beautifully, and then had a copy of it framed for each child's room. The statement concludes, "The best birthright we can give you is our love. Our love is our blessing on your life. Our love is your assurance that you have never been and will never be a mistake in our eyes. Our love is the most precious gift we can give you—and we give it freely because you are the most precious gift ever given to us!"

One mother worked the message into a birth-record piece of cross-stitched embroidery: "7 pounds and 1 ounce of pure love."

One father wore a T-shirt with this message on the front: "Go ahead. Make my day. Ask me how much I love my children."

Your love is the best gift you can ever give your child. More than anything else, your love gives your child a feeling of security, a foundation for healthy self-esteem, and good mental and emotional health throughout his or her life.

2 ✦ Meet Your Child's Basic Needs

Before your child can ever truly believe you when you say "I love you," your child must know that you are vitally concerned about meeting his or her basic needs. These needs include nourishment, shelter, and safety.

Nourishment Children need nutritional foods prepared in nutritional ways. They need pure drinking water. "But my children don't like certain foods," you may say. Train them to like them. Serve a wide variety of foods. Prepare them in the simplest ways possible: raw, steamed, baked, broiled. Let children experience the fullness of flavors without layers of salt, chemical preservatives, or oils.

Children's minds also require nourishment. Children need exposure to a wide variety of stimuli that will trigger their creativity, spark their imaginations, and promote their developing sense of values. They need experiences more than they need toys. They need play time more than they need media time. They need opportunities for relating with other children and adults.

This does not mean that you need to overload your child with flashcards and schooling at an early age or that you need to create a toy-store atmosphere in your child's room. To a child, the cupboard with pots and pans holds great creative potential. The backyard can be jungle, forest, or beach—the back porch a fortress, palace, or dungeon. The opportunity to be with you in the kitchen as you prepare a meal may be the best lesson of the day.

- Ask yourself, "Does the toy I'm providing stimulate creativity?
- Ask yourself, "Does this activity promote the values and mental growth that I want to see in my child?"

Shelter *Children also need shelter.* As a basic need, they require protection from the harshness of their environment. A child's environment encompasses more than the weather.

Mothers who would never dream of sending their children out to play in the snow without mittens and hats often fail to see a threat in the constant din of noise outside their city window. Children need quiet. They need to know that they can shut off and shut out the world.

Children need warmth when it is cold and cool shelter from the heat. They need to be able to get into their own homes using door latches that are within reach and doors that they can open easily. They need to be able to get to a glass of cold water without asking for permission or help. They need to be able to take off a layer of clothing or add a layer.

Children need space. They need to have a corner of the world they can *call* their own, in which they are free to create a world *of* their own. For some, it may be a bed of their own. For others, it may be a room of their own, the bottom of a small closet, or a treehouse.

Safety   Children need freedom from pain. They need to know that their parents are doing everything possible to keep them healthy. One of the best ways to be sure you are meeting your child's basic needs is to make regular trips to a pediatrician. Have your child's hearing and eyesight checked periodically. Regular dental care also falls into this category.

Children also need freedom from emotional and mental pain. They need to be sheltered from abusive situations.

Note that the emphasis here is on needs, not wants. You do *not* have a responsibility to provide for all of your child's *wants.* You do *not* have a responsibility to provide the best, most elaborate products, services, or environment possible. A modest house can be just as much a home as a mansion. A pair of jeans wears just as well *without* a designer label.

The root of love is not emotion, it is provision. By providing for your child's basic needs, you are establishing a foundation on which love has meaning. Meet your child's basic needs, and your expressions of love will be all your child ever needs in addition.

3 ✦ Nicknames

A nickname, a term of endearment, is one of the easiest ways to express your love to your child on a daily basis. For my brother and me, the names were simply "Jannie" and "Craigie." The names look strange in print, but they never sounded strange to our ears. They were what Mommy and Daddy called us.

Nicknames—special, affectionate, private names—are a wonderful bonding device when they are used in a loving way.

Make a nickname an endearing signal of a loving relationship unique to your child. Don't call anyone else by that name. A nickname says to a child, "You're extra special to me. I have a name for you that embodies my love. It's a name I use *only* for you!"

Privacy *A loving nickname is best used in privacy.* It is almost as good as a secret code name. It says to the world, "There's a relationship here that's private and closed to the outside world."

- Always make certain that your child is comfortable with the nickname.

    When possible, adopt something of the

child's initial choosing, perhaps something they called themselves or by which they have identified themselves. You might ask your child, "Who are you to me?" (This question can be a revealing one on many levels. Be prepared for an eye-opening answer.)

• Don't use a nickname that embarrasses your child either personally or in public.

Avoid nicknames that refer to physical traits or family standing. The child nicknamed "Baby" won't like that nickname once he has grown to be six feet tall and starts to shave. "Junior" describes a relationship; it is not a true nickname. And no child wants to be called "Boopsie" once she hits puberty. If a child says, "Don't call me *that*" . . . then, don't.

Continuity Nicknames used over the months and years give a child a sense of consistency in a relationship. I was Jannie forty years ago. I'm still Jannie today. My nickname suggests continuity, long-standing affection, and a sense of confidence that "I'm sombody" on the inside, even if the outside world never knows it.

A nickname used over the years and decades becomes a synonym for "unique and wonderful." And in that, there's love!

4 ✦ Read with Your Child

One of the easiest and most cherished ways of spending time with your child is to read with your child. Reading together creates a closed unit. For those few minutes in a day, your child knows that she has your undivided attention. She also knows, as she sits close to you or on your lap, that the two of you are virtually impervious to outside demands.

Read Aloud to Your Child Even when your child is still in the crib, read! Let your child experience the way that you put words together, the inflections that you use, the different character voices that you adopt. Let your child delight in a variety of stories. Choose books for your young child that trigger his or her imagination.

As your child grows older, let your child help with the choosing. Make visits to the library a regular part of your family routine.

Here are some pointers for reading together:

- Hold your child close. Let him know that you are not only eager to share mind to mind, but that you desire to be in close proximity.
- Personalize a story whenever you can. Point out

things in illustrations that may not be a part of the story. Ask your child questions: *"What do you think will happen next?" "Which one of these do you like best?" "Have you ever felt this way?"*

- Move at a pace that is comfortable to your child. She will let you know when you are going too fast or too slow. Stopping you from turning a page means, "Not so fast, Dad. Slow down. I need more time with this page—and with you." Fidgeting means, "Read faster, Mom." Flipping ahead to the next page means, "I don't have enough attention span to listen to all of this. Cut to the chase."

Let Your Child Read Aloud to You   Value what your child reads to you. Listen attentively. Sit side by side. Ask questions when they seem appropriate, but stop asking if your child reprimands you for interrupting. Don't fret over words read incorrectly. Help your child with words only if he asks for your help. He's looking for love, not education.

One young father I know wanted to have a reading time with his children but, as a farmer who was up and at work by 4 A.M., he was often too tired to stay awake beyond the first few pages of a story. He finally resorted to stories on tape. He would lie on one of the children's beds with the tape deck on his stomach and a child tucked under each arm. Together, they listened to tales serious and humorous. A few times his children had to awaken him to have him turn over the tape, but these reading sessions were filled with love and closeness.

Make reading times a regular part of your daily schedule.

- Capture a few moments while dinner is cooking to sit down with your child and read. Reading is a great way to help a child unwind from play and settle down for a quiet evening.
- You may want to read with your child after bath-time and before bedtime, as a cozy transition toward a peaceful night.

Bear in mind that just as your child is never too young for a reading time, so your child is never too old. Your teenager might not sit as close to you, but you can still enjoy the intimacy of a story shared together.

As your children grow older, have nights when the living room becomes a reading room—with everybody reading. Be willing to be interrupted by a child who finds a passage too humorous to keep to himself. Be willing to share what you find to be of special interest.

Books provide fertile ground for parent-child relationships. And in that ground, love grows exceedingly well.

5 ✦ Make Something Together

Your child will always understand love expressed in terms of time spent together. One of the best ways of spending time together is to make something together.

The point of the exercise is this: do it *together*. Don't choose an activity in which you are doing the making and your child is doing the watching. Also avoid activities in which your child is doing the making and you are doing the supervising.

Things to Do   What are some good things to do together? Here are four neutral, evenly shared activities for you to consider.

Cooking. You chop up one ingredient. Let your child chop up another. You make the cake. Let your child make the frosting. You make the meat dish. Let your child make the salad. You turn the crank for homemade ice cream. Let your child watch the meat on the grill.

Gardening. You plant one row. Let your child plant the adjacent row. You weed one patch. Let your child weed another. You pick the tomatoes. Let your child harvest the zucchini.

Doing jigsaw puzzles. Work on one part of the puzzle as your child works on another. You find a piece; your child finds a piece.

Making models. (This includes dollhouses, birdhouses, train sets, and so forth.) You paint some of the pieces. Let your child paint the others. Paper one wall of the dollhouse while your child papers another. Hold pieces for each other while the glue sets.

How to Work Together In working together, follow a few simple rules to keep the activity loving and not confrontational.

- *Be willing to accept your child's work.* Allow for imperfections. Be willing for the carrot slices to be of varying thickness. Be willing for the glue to ooze out around some pieces.
- *Choose something that you both regard as important or fun.* Don't insist that your child build a model airplane when he would rather be putting together a model ship. Let your child help choose the puzzle and help decide what to do with it after it is finished (such as frame it, pull it apart, give it away, make a mosaic-style tray out of it).
- *Whenever possible, choose activities that don't have a deadline or a tight time frame.* Make this a relaxed time to be together. If a child feels the pressure of time, he is likely to make even more mistakes than he might normally, which will make the activity less fun for him. Don't expect your child to be as quick as you are at a task.

- *Don't make this activity an excuse for conversation.* Many parents choose to do something with their child as a way of starting a conversation or in hopes that their child will open up to them on an important topic. Your child may; she may not.
- *Praise your child for the work he does.* Let him know you value his effort, his skill, his accomplishment. *"Good job." "Thanks." "You know, we're really getting good at this."*
- *Let your child know you are happy to be with him.* Say, *"You know, I'd rather be doing this with you than just about anybody I can think of." "I like digging potatoes with you." "You're a good sport to be doing this with me."*
- *Choose an activity that has an end.* Dinner eventually gets on the table. The gardening is eventually over for the day or the season. The puzzle gets finished. The glue dries and the model is put up on the shelf. The dollhouse is finally finished and ready for play.

The beauty or success of the thing you have made is not what your child will remember or praise. The time that you have spent together and the fact that you have made something together are what will be remembered as examples of your love shared.

6 ✦ Sign Language

Learn to say "I love you" in your own personal sign language. That way, you can send your message even across a crowded room.

In the language of the deaf, "I love you" is generally expressed in these three hand motions:

Point to yourself.   Cross your heart.   Point to the other person.

Private Messages You don't need to use large motions to convey the message, however. There are times when you should "whisper" your message, even when using signals. Be discreet and aware of your child's reactions. You can always point to your heart and cross it with just a finger and then nod to the other person with a wink. That's the way one mother sent encouragement to her children as they were up on stage preparing to sing a song in the church Christmas pageant.

Creative Messages   Encourage your child to be creative in the ways he expresses the "I love you" message. One young boy I know pointed to his mouth instead of to his heart. He then grinned broadly, all of his front teeth showing, and held his finger up closely to his mouth to point at his grandfather. In his own sign language, he was probably conveying, "I smile you" or "I grin you." In truth, he was saying, "I love you, Grandpa!"

Another young child rubbed her heart area instead of crossing it. She rubbed and rubbed, with a great look of seriousness, almost pain, on her face. I asked, "What are you saying with all that rubbing?" She answered, "I love you lots and lots and *lots.*"

Many times parents find themselves too far away to give an encouraging word. What do you say when your child stares back frantically from the front row just moments before he is to perform in his first piano recital? What do you do as your child prepares to march onto the football field in her first appearance as a majorette?

Use sign language. Others may be able to "overhear" what you say, but nobody will be embarrassed by your message, including your child.

7 ✦ Keep Your Child's Secrets

Love is based on trust. Your child must be able to trust your words as being true. Your child must be able to trust that you are *always* concerned that his needs are met. Your child must be able to trust that you will *always* be her ally.

Your child's trust can be gained, in part, by keeping your child's secrets. On the other hand, nothing can destroy your child's trust in you faster than by your betraying his confidence.

Must you keep all of your child's secrets? Yes. You do, however, have the prerogative of defining what a secret may or may *not* be.

When Secrets Are Something Else Share with your child the difference between a piece of information and a secret. Only allow your child to classify as secrets those things that are about himself and himself alone. You cannot and must not be responsible for secrets about other children.

Teach your child the difference between telling a secret and making an admission of guilt. Just because your child tells you something and says that it is in confidence doesn't mean that he can't be punished for it. "If I tell you a secret, will you promise not to be mad, Mom?" asks your child. Don't agree! You may be stuck with an admission such as, "I just picked all the daisies in Mrs. Smith's yard."

When Secrets Are Implied Many of the things your child does should also be considered a secret by you, even if that word is never used or your child doesn't ask you to keep something a secret. The world doesn't need to know when your daughter starts wearing a bra. The entire neighborhood doesn't need to hear from you that your son just kissed a girlfriend for the first time.

Even your best friend doesn't need to know the intimate conversations you may have with your child about his problems, her questions, his fears, her decisions.

Children retell their own secrets. Don't be surprised to discover that you aren't the only one who has been told something in the highest confidence. Very often, a child will tell you something as a secret only to see how you will react, what you will say, and to test the waters of adult opinion on a subject, incident, or idea.

By keeping your child's secrets in confidence, you are saying, "Your trust is precious to me, so precious I won't willingly do anything to destroy it." Trust creates an atmosphere in which love is freely expressed and freely received; it is the atmosphere in which the words "I love you" are spoken with the greatest validity.

8 ✦ Require Honesty of Feelings

Don't cover up your feelings. Don't allow your child to cover up his. When you are angry or disappointed or hurt, say so. When you are happy, excited, or satisfied, say so.

A child who hears honest emotions from an adult comes to appreciate honest emotions and is more willing to express them. Why is honesty of emotions important? Because you want your child to believe you when you express your deepest, highest, and ultimate emotion: "I have a heart bursting with love for you!"

Personhood Versus Deeds Emotional reactions are generally very specific reactions to what someone has said or done. It is important for your child to hear you make a distinction between how you feel about a person and how you feel about that person's behavior in a specific instance.

- "I'm so happy that I got a raise. This means that my boss is happy with my work, and I like knowing that I'm doing a good job. This also means that we'll have a little more money to spend. I like that fact, too!"

- "I'm really disappointed that I didn't get to go on the trip. I was looking forward to seeing London. But I realize that Daddy had to go alone this time and that it was a work trip, not a vacation."
- "I'm very angry that you picked all of Mrs. Smith's flowers. That was a mean and naughty thing to do. I want you to go to your room, and I'll be in shortly to punish you."

By making statements such as these you are separating your feelings about certain actions, decisions, or behavior from the personhood of your boss, your husband, or your child.

What would be the result, however, if one said, *"I'm so happy. I've got the greatest boss in the world."* The implication is that the boss is the cause of happiness. Your child doesn't know what the boss did to cause your happiness, only that your boss and happiness are related. An emotion becomes linked to a person, not to that person's behavior.

"I'm so disappointed. Daddy gets to go and I don't." The implication is that Daddy is responsible for the disappointment. Daddy is so closely linked to disappointment that it is not a far reach for a child to conclude that Daddy is a disappointment.

"I'm so angry. You are a naughty boy." The action isn't separated from the child. Naughty now? Naughty always? Naughty for this? Or, naughty as a character trait?

It is important for your child to know that you love

him for *who he is,* even though you may not always like *what he does.* Otherwise, your love becomes deed-bound. Your child will forever be trying to earn your love or win your love. He will feel he must *do* something to deserve your love or be worthy of your love. A child needs to know that he *has* your love and your devotion but that his *deeds* may, at times, have your disapproval.

Only as your child understands that deeds and personhood are separate will he be able to differentiate punishment for deeds from punishment for character. If your child knows he is being punished for his misdeeds, he can learn to change those deeds— which is the reason for punishment in the first place.

Love Versus Qualifications for Love Tell your child what you like about other people. But keep love separate from qualifications whenever possible.

"I love you because you are my son. That's the most special love in the world. There's nothing like it. It just is. I love you because of who you are."

"I love you because you are my daughter. You're one of a kind and totally unique to me, and my love for you isn't like anything I've ever felt for anyone else. I love you just because you are you."

Those statements will be perceived as honest ones only if you are honest about the way you feel at other times. Give your child words and emotions he can trust.

9 ✦ Freely Forgive

Nothing frees a child more to experience your love than for you to forgive your child. Children know at a fairly early age when they have done something to earn their parents' disapproval.

Sin is a serious word, not one to be taken lightly. It is important for you to discuss with your child the difference between *sins* and *mistakes.*

Mistakes Mistakes are things your child does accidentally in the course of trying to do right or good things. Mistakes also are made when children don't focus their attention on what they are doing, when they are trying to do something for the first time and as they practice a skill. Mistakes are often made in the course of a child's seeking to have fun.

The new shoes are ruined as the result of the child's stomping through too many puddles. The glass of milk is knocked over as the child, trying to be independent, reaches for the bowl of olives. The skirt is ripped as the child climbs over a fence in an effort to get home on time.

Mistakes generally result in some type of damage to people or things or events. Sins, on the other hand, are those willful acts that breach or cause damage to a relationship.

Sins   Unrepented and unforgiven sins shut down communication, destroy trust, cause guilt, and, ultimately, create a false sense of reality in the child's mind.

Lying, cheating (and other acts of dishonesty), and *stealing* are common childhood sins. Indeed, children seem to have an inbred ability to commit them from toddlerhood on.

The problem with sins is that they compound. One sinful act tends to breed another. What's a parent to do?

- *It is the responsibility of the parent to confront the child with his sins.* Mistakes are generally obvious to all, and confrontation is rarely necessary. Sins are often more subtle. Let your child know that you know that he has done something to breach your trust and to muddy the waters of your communication and the close loving relationship that you value dearly.
- *It is the responsibility of the parent to hear the child's full confession.* Don't react too quickly. Make sure you hear the whole story. Don't allow your child to confess only half of what he did or admit to only half of what she didn't do. Don't move toward punishment too quickly. Hear your child out. Look for underlying motives. Probe a little.

- *It is the responsibility of the parent to punish sin.*
Sin has consequences. That is part of what
makes it sin. If the consequences don't come
from you at an early age, they will come from
someone else at some other time, and usually
with far more severity.

  Mistakes are also punishable, especially for
acts in which the child has been forewarned
(and thus, the mistake is an act of disobedience)
or for acts in which the error could have been
avoided by forethought. Punishment is a means
of training a child not to do certain deeds again.
Punishments for mistakes, however, can generally be less severe than those administered for
sin because mistakes are generally more
quickly recognized.

  What type of punishment is best? Simply put,
a punishment should be something your child
doesn't want. There is no perfect punishment
that works for all children. It may be a spanking.
It may be foregoing a planned outing.
- *It is the parent's responsibility to forgive the child.*
Punishment is aimed at the deed of the child.
Forgiveness is aimed at the guilt and the stain
on the relationship.

Don't wink at your child's sins. Give your child the
freedom of spirit that comes through confrontation,
repentance, an appropriate punishment, and your
freely given forgiveness. That says to a child, "I love
you enough to care about who you become."

10 ✦ Let Your Child Know You Didn't Make a Mistake

Children need to feel wanted in order for them to feel truly loved. Very often, children draw a conclusion from a parent's momentary indifference or temporary neglect that Mommy doesn't want me around or that Daddy doesn't care if I live or die.

Your young child lives in the moment and from moment to moment. He can hear from you five times a day that you love him and he won't grow tired of it.

As your child grows older, he requires less frequent telling. Your relationship has more time built into it. Trust runs deeper. He is more sure of your presence and your love.

Nevertheless, it is important periodically to assure your child that she is wanted, that you wouldn't trade her for the world (and several planets and stars), and that you don't even like to think about how drab life would be without her.

One of the most cherished letters I ever received from my mother was one in which she described an afternoon ride she and my father had taken up into the mountains. They had spent several hours exploring this road and that one. Mom wrote, "We talked about whether we would do it all over again if we knew then what we know now, and we decided that, yes, we would." By "doing it all over again" she was referring to their marriage and their decision to have children. Even at age twenty-two, I felt a warm glow in reading her letter. I had never suspected that I was unwanted. In fact, I was quite sure during all my growing-up years that I had been very much wanted as a baby and that I was very much wanted, appreciated, and loved as a child. Still, it was nice to have it confirmed one more time.

- Tell your child that you are glad he was born. Convey to your child, *"I'm glad you're alive. I'm glad you're you. I'm glad you're here."*
- Let your son know that you are glad he was born *your son.* Let your daughter know that you are glad she was born *your daughter.*
- Let your adopted child know that if you had to do the choosing again, you would make the same choice.
- Let your child know he was an answer to prayer, that she was your heart's desire.

Give your child the assurance that you have wanted him, you do want him, and that you will always want him. That is the best foundation for love that you can establish.

11 ✦ Keep a Special Place for Memories of Your Child

Have a special place where you keep photos and other momentos about your child. Have a special place, too, where you record your feelings and memories about your child. Let your child know that he is so precious to you that you want to cherish every minute of his life.

Your special place may be . . .

- a drawer.
- a cupboard.
- a large wooden box.
- a trunk or chest.
- an album, journal, or scrapbook.

Ellen kept a journal during her pregnancy to record, on a periodic basis, how she was feeling about the child developing within her womb. She wrote about how she felt when she first heard the news that she was pregnant and about how excited she was the day she heard the baby's heartbeat. She told about how she felt the first time the baby kicked inside her. After her son was born, she wrote in great detail about her feelings, the reactions of his father and grandparents, and her hopes and dreams for her child, that he might grow up to be a loving, generous, sensitive man.

Jerry wrote about life with his toddler, Rachel, in a small book he titled simply, "Rachel of Heather Cottage"—Heather Cottage being the name they had given to their home. He wrote about the funny things she did and said and about his feelings as a father during those early growing-up years. What a gift beyond price to Rachel.

Things to Do   Write little notes alongside the photos in your album telling something about the events, special memories, and feelings.

Keep your child's love notes. Tuck them into your Bible or into a box designated just for that purpose.

Keep sample Christmas cards, especially the ones with photos of your children on them, for each of your children's scrapbooks.

Love Means Being a Pack Rat   Your child equates his things with himself. "Mine!" must certainly be one of the Top Ten First Words every child learns. When your child sees you valuing his things—his little drawings, his notes, his awards, his newspaper clippings, photos of himself—he begins to believe, "Mom loves my stuff. Mom loves me. Daddy is proud of my creations and accomplishments. Daddy is proud of me."

12 ✦ Get Down on Your Child's Level

Stoop. Kneel. Crawl. Sit. Lie down on the floor. Do whatever it takes to get down on your child's level at least once a day. You will discover a number of things as you see the world through your child's eyes.

New Discoveries

- *You'll realize how big and how frightening some things can be.* Close your eyes and imagine how big your dining table would have to be if it was built in proportion to your *present* height.

  Imagine staring a dog in the eye and knowing that he weighs twice as much as you do and has four legs instead of your two.

  Imagine staring up at an angry person who is more than twice your height and having that person wave in your direction a wooden spoon that is half your height.

  Imagine sitting atop a ten-foot stool. That is proportionately how your child feels as he sits in his high chair. It's a long way down to that floor.

- *You'll realize what an incomplete view your child*

has of the world. One year I decided to take a young friend out for a look at the Christmas lights in our city, only to realize after he was all buckled into the front seat of my little red car that he couldn't see out the windows!

Your child may be able to look up and see the stained glass windows as you sit together in church. He may be able to look around and see bodies of adults. But chances are, he can't see the preacher or the altar.

I recently took a couple of young friends to a children's theater performance. The audience was enthusiastic, the play exciting, and the standing ovation given at the conclusion of the final act a rousing one. Suddenly I felt a tug at my skirt and heard three mournful words: "I can't see!"

- *You'll realize how unstimulating much of the world seems with all of the "good stuff" placed way too high.* Imagine a world that looks like the front of your sofa, the edge of the bed, the lower half of your kitchen cabinets, or the enamel of your kitchen appliances.

    Paintings are nearly always hung too high for a young child to enjoy them. The prettiest and most enticing things are nearly always "up there" out of reach.

- *You'll realize how out of control you really are as a child.* Faucets and door knobs and door bells are all out of reach. Toilets are too big. Clothes are hung on closet rods that are too high. In order to get or do many of the essential things in life, you've got to have help. Crawl around in your child's world for awhile, and you will have a new appreciation for some of his frustrations and fears.

New Opportunities With your new awareness of how your child sees his or her environment, you will have new opportunities to stimulate your child's creativity. Take time to point out some things to your child. Help him notice things you would like for him to recognize in his world.

Take some props from the upper world down to your child's level with you. Let your child feel and hold items as he sits three inches from the floor. This not only gives your child a sense of control and encourages his creativity, but there is less chance the item will break if it is dropped.

You will have a new opportunity to play with your child. Let your child know that you can have fun in her world, just as you anticipate that she will have fun in yours. You will have a new opportunity to tell your child, "I love you."

There is no more effective way of telling your child "I love you" than by telling him eye-to-eye. Often we pull children up to our level. We lift them up on our laps or into our arms or let them stand on their bed to tell them we love them. Try getting down on your child's level and telling him from that vantage point. He will *know* you mean it.

13 ✦ Find Something to Do for Mutual Fun

Find something to do with your child that you *both* enjoy doing. And then spend time with your child doing that thing. Fun with you and time with you—your child will feel a double dose of love.

Key Ingredients There are five key ingredients for having a successful fun time with your child.

- *Make certain the activity is something you both enjoy doing.* If you are doing something only because your child enjoys it, you'll get tired of it easily and you won't want to do it. The result is that you won't do it or you will resent doing it. The same holds true for your child.
- *Make certain the activity is not something that you enable your child to do but that you truly both do.* Don't just hold the jumprope so your son can jump. Don't look over your daughter's shoulder while she takes on Ms. PacMan at the video arcade. Don't just watch while your child rides the carousel.
- *Make certain that the activity doesn't hurt either*

one of you, physically or emotionally. When children and adults play tag football together, guess who most often gets hurt? When you carry a child on your shoulders the length of the entire mall, guess who has the sore neck?

Parents often find themselves competing with their children as they play with them. It may be inadvertent or subconcious. It is competition, nonetheless. Children don't enjoy losing or being embarrassed any more than adults do. If you are going to play a competitive game with your child, make sure it is a game in which your child (with a fairly high percentage of probability) can win.

- *Don't get locked into an activity. Stay flexible with it.* Watch your child at play with his peers. They can move from one game to the next with hardly a blink of the eye. They can play out a dozen different scenarios in the course of an afternoon at the park. Children frequently don't finish a board game or play all the innings. Don't insist that your child finish every game you begin. (Insist sometimes, not all the time.)

  Don't insist that your child always play by the rules. Children like to make up their own rules. Of course, you may insist that once they make up the rules, they don't change them midstream. At the same time, recognize that very few games have rules that can't be altered.

- *Find an activity that gives you room to laugh.* Having fun with your child is a *process,* not an accomplishment. Fun is marked by laughter, a sense of play, a delight in the doing. Fun is marked by pleasure. If you or your child can't laugh along the way, and if you feel no pleasure in the sheer act of *doing* something, don't do it. It's just not fun.

What to Do   So what can you do with your child that is fun, enjoyed mutually, not harmful to either one of you, and which you can both do without a time frame or omnipresent goal? Ask your child! You can say to your child, "Tell me the top ten things you like to do most in the whole world."

Chances are, there will be at least one of your child's Top Ten Things to Do that you like to do or think you might like to try. If not, ask your child for another batch of things she likes to do. Even if you settle for the eighteenth activity on her list, you may be surprised that by doing it together, and having fun together, that activity quickly moves into your child's Top Ten.

It is your time, your attention, and your laughter shared only with him that your child craves. A mutually enjoyed and mutually exclusive time together is a surefire way of saying, "I want to be with you. I love you."

14 ✦ Just Say So

Gather up all your courage. Take the time. Find a private moment. And mean it when you say it. But most importantly, give voice to the words "I love you."

It's Not Always Easy

- *Sometimes it takes courage to tell a child you love him.* The older a child grows, the more many parents feel the potential for their child to reject them. A shrug of the shoulders from a teen hurts just as much as from a spouse or a boss or a pastor. Rejection is rejection is rejection. That's the time when you need to muster your courage. Say, "I love you" even if you get a bad reaction or no reaction.
- *Telling your child you love him takes time and privacy.* A casually tossed, "I love you" will be perceived as a casually tossed emotion.

  Don't try to tell your child you love him when he is with his friends—or with anybody else, for that matter. Find a private moment.

  Find a moment when your statement isn't linked to anything your child has won or earned. Saying "I love you" after your child is named class president sends a subtle message to your child, "Dad loves me *because* I'm class president." Your child needs to know that you love him because he is your son and for no other reason.

- *Mean it when you say it.* Your child has built-in radar for insincerity. Your child knows when your words ring with a hollow sound.

You may not feel a great emotional surge in saying "I love you" to your child. Many times emotions run deeper than words.

Love Is for Always   Always keep in mind that love is more than a feeling. It is a declaration of your will, your desire, your state of being quite apart from your emotions. Emotions tend to be rooted in "now." Love is rooted in "always." You can *mean* something, even if you don't feel your heart jumping hurdles. Don't confuse the feeling of love with the *fact* of love. Assure your child that you love him as a undeniable, irrefutable, unchangeable fact of your life.

Don't assume that your child is so confident of your love that he will be annoyed at your saying the words. No child ever gets tired of hearing "I love you" from a parent who means what he says and who chooses the right time and place to say so.

15 ✦ Give Thanks for Your Child in Times of Prayer

Pray for your child. Let your child hear your thanksgiving to God for him or her. Nothing conveys a more intimate or deeper sense of your love.

"God loves you and I do, too." That is a good thought to convey to your child often. Confirm that truth for both God and your child to hear.

> *Thank you, Lord, for sending Jessica to our family to be our daughter. We know that she is Your precious child and she is our precious child, too.*

Thank God for the many wonderful traits of your child.

> *Heavenly Father, we're so grateful that You have sent Billy to be a part of our family. We marvel every day at the way in which You have created him.*

Thank God for your child's accomplishments.

> *Thank You, Lord, for helping Paul to score two goals in his soccer game today. Thank You for giv-*

ing him such a strong body and the energy to run and play so well.

Thank God for your child's acts of courage and moral bravery.

Heavenly Father, I thank You that You helped Kirsten to do what was right today, to tell the truth even though it was hard to do. Thank You for giving her the courage not to tell a lie.

Thank God for your child's friends, teachers, and family members.

Thank you, heavenly Father, for giving Colton such a good T-ball coach and for giving him friends to play ball with. Thank You, too, for letting Joe's nursery sponsor the team.

Lord, we're grateful that Aunt Sue can come visit us for a few days. Please give her a safe trip and help us to have a good time with her while she's here. We know she loves us all. Help us to show her how much we love her. Thank you that she is our Aunt Sue.

Thank God for protecting your child and for giving her health.

Father, thank You for keeping Carolina safe as she played today. Thank You for giving her such good health. Thank You for helping her remember to brush her teeth without my having to remind her.

You can't always be with your child. And no parent knows how many days, months, or years she has with her child. Keep your child's heart open to receiving God's love.

Ask God to help your child with his or her problems and needs.

Lord God, I ask You tonight to help Tammi know what to do and what to say to her friend Brenda. Give her the courage to speak up and to be able to tell Brenda how she feels about Brenda's rebellious attitude toward her parents.

In your times of prayer with your child, ask God to help you be a loving parent.

Heavenly Father, thank You for letting Carla be our daughter. Help me to be a good parent to her. Help me to find new ways to show her how much I love her and appreciate her.

Finally, give your child an opportunity to pray for you. When you are down or facing a problem at work or are feeling ill or are tired, ask your child to pray for you. Let your child know that her prayers count.

Prayer times with your child may well be the most intimate times you will ever share with your child. Make the most of them in conveying your love and God's love to your child.

16 ✦ Hugs and Kisses

Nearly every child loves to be hugged and kissed, even if he won't admit it. Hugs and kisses are an important way to express your love to your child.

Try letting your child—or teen—know that you need a hug. You may be surprised at how willing he is to give one to you!

Hugs and kisses convey to your child that you appreciate his or her physical personhood. Young children see themselves in terms of their bodies. They don't yet have a well-developed concept of their own minds or spirits, although they certainly use them and operate out of them. They do know, however, that they have toes and arms.

Some parents wonder just how much of a hug to give. Here are some simple rules:

- Let the child hug *you* as much as you hug him. Don't hug your child beyond what he or she is comfortable hugging you back.

  Some children are clingers. They can drape themselves around your neck for fifteen minutes and they never seem to grow tired of being held. Other children are blitzers. They are willing to hug you for all of five seconds and then they are off to their next activity. (Blitzers do often come around for a dozen five-second hugs, however.) Don't try to cling to a blitzer, and don't try to blitz a clinger.

- Be aware of each child's need, mood, and means of expressing his love to you.

   Don't insist on hugging a child if she doesn't want to be hugged. If the child says no—either in words or body language—accept that as her mood of the moment and respond simply, "Well, maybe later." Don't force a hug.

- Keep kisses light and playful.

   Should you kiss a child on the mouth? Probably not, unless it's your own son or daughter. And then, only if your child is comfortable with that kind of kiss. Children will often spontaneously kiss you with a giant, slobbery on-the-mouth variety. Accept that with a "Wow, what did I do to deserve that" attitude.

- When a child hits puberty, shift to shoulder hugs. Or wrap your arms around your child's shoulders or waist from the back as he or she is slouching in the sofa or sitting on a bench.

Above all, keep your hugging and kissing innocent and not insistent, but keep those hugs and kisses coming. Your child needs to know, always, as a primary need, that you like his physical personhood. A child whose parents reject his or her body as untouchable will have a difficult time hearing their words, "I love you."

17 ✦ Give Flowers to Your Child

The giving of flowers conveys a strong message of love, in our culture and in that of many others. Flowers can express

- *love in times of celebration.*
- *love in the depths of grief.*
- *love in terms of appreciation.*

Give your child flowers from an early age. He or she will look back later and say, "Hmmm . . . flowers mean love in this world. Mom and Dad always gave them to me. Mom and Dad loved me then and love me now."

Give flowers to both your son and daughter. Don't discriminate. Glenda once said to her teenage son when she spontaneously brought home a bouquet of daisies to him: "This is an example of 'do unto others as you would have them do unto you.' As a woman, not just as your mother, I'm giving you these flowers as a lesson in what *every* woman you'll ever meet will enjoy receiving from you."

Use flowers as a way of cultivating in your child an appreciation for beauty. Point out beautiful gardens to your child as you drive through the neighborhoods of your city. Point out beautiful flowers as you take a walk with your child. That way your gift of flowers will not only be a love gift, but a gift of beauty.

- Surprise your child with flowers.

  Robert didn't expect to come home from school to find a big bouquet of roses in his very, very messy room. The note on them said, "I love you —even if I can't stand to be in your room."

  Robert's mother came home from work late that evening to find, as she peeked into her son's room to say goodnight, a much cleaner room. And in her own room she found one of the roses with a note to her: "I love you, too, Mom!"

  Shari didn't expect flowers as she finished her first piano lesson. "Concert pianists usually get flowers after they've finished a performance," her mother explained. "I don't expect you to be a concert pianist, but I do hope you'll always enjoy your own performances at the piano."

- Give flowers to your child on the same occasions in which you would consider giving flowers to an adult.

  After his dog died, Troy found a garden bouquet in his room. The note said simply, "I'm sorry. Love, Mom."

  When Lisa turned sixteen, she received a bouquet of a dozen pink roses, delivered to her at school. "Happy birthday, sweetheart. Love, Dad and Mother."

- Give your child a plant or tree or bush that can then be transplanted into your garden. Let your child help with the transplanting. Andy received a tree as a gift the day after he had finally reached the four-foot mark on the height chart posted on the back of his bedroom door. "You're really growing up, son. Let's help something else grow up, too. Love, Dad." Father and son planted the tree together and both parents noted that Andy frequently referred to it as his tree. Nearly twenty years later Andy told his six-year-old daughter during a visit to Grandma's and Grandpa's house, "See that tree? That's my four-foot tree. When you hit four feet, we're going to plant a tree together in *our* yard!"

In our family we had azalea row. I can walk alongside it and say, "There's the one that Mom got from Dad when I was born . . . and that's the one that I gave Mom for her fiftieth birthday . . . and this is the one that we received when Grandpa died." That azalea bed is more than beautiful; it's history.

Flowers help underscore certain events for your child. They make certain moments more memorable. Flowers give your child a tangible, visual example of your love. Share them generously.

18 ✦ Be Willing to Let Go

Two of the greatest things any parent can ever give a child are a firm foundation of love and wings.

- Encourage your child to explore his world. As a parent, you have the prerogative to set boundaries and limits for your child, but within those boundaries, allow your child to explore freely.

  The boundary may be the backyard fence. The boundary lines may be "from the bench to the tree to the sandbox" at the park. The boundary may be "our block."

- Provide adventure books for your child, especially biographies of explorers, missionaries, travelers, adventurers. Give wings to your child's imagination. Let your child know, *"There's nobody I'd rather share the world with than you. I want you to have the freedom to pursue your interests and to fully explore your world."*

- Encourage your child to have relationships with children her age as well as with other caring adults. Give your child "permission" to love others and to create memories that don't include you.

- Encourage your child to explore his own potential and to take risks of creativity, effort, and of giving.

Alice had wanted to take skiing lessons for as long as anyone could remember. Alice's mother was frightened to let her daughter out on the slopes, since she herself had broken her leg as a child while learning to ski. Alice did just fine.

When Paul asked if he could try out for the boy's choir, his parents were astonished. They had never heard him sing. In fact, they had been told by a kindergarten teacher that Paul was tone deaf. "Are you sure?" asked Mother. "Yes," said Paul. "It's something I want to try." He did. He made the choir. He was even given a solo part at a concert.

One of your main responsibilities as an adult is to prepare your child to leave home one day. Incorporate statements such as these into your conversations:

- "When you visit that nation some day . . ."
- "I can hardly wait to see how you'll decorate your own apartment someday . . ."
- "In case you have to travel someday in your business or your job . . ."

Use these phrases as you teach your child important skills, from cooking to repairing to ordering food to packing to sewing.

When your child rebels against a rule you have

established or questions your abilities as a parent, you can always say:

- "Someday when you are an adult and out on your own, you may choose to . . ."

Children's security is not rooted in their being tied to your apron strings; it is in knowing that they have the freedom to be with you and the freedom to be on their own.

"One of the sounds that I miss most since Joe left for college is the sound of the screen door slamming," said his mother Gladys. "Very early on, Ed and I decided that we would put a low latch on the screen door so that Joe could always come and go from the house as he wanted. That way we weren't interrupted, and he wasn't inhibited. He must have gone in and out of the house a hundred times a day. We did require, of course, that he kill every fly that he let in! We felt it was important that Joe know that we were always here when he needed us, but that at the same time, we expected him to go out and make a mark on the world."

It is your job as a parent to train up your child to assume an adult role in our society. Wean your child. Encourage his growth and independence. Letting go is one of the most loving things you will ever do for your child.

19 ✦ A Note of Surprise

Tuck a little surprise message into a corner of your child's life. Say "I love you" in a moment when your child least expects it.

It might be a note glued to the bottom of the lunchbox: *"Hi. I ♥ you!"*

It might be a note tucked into a sock in the suitcase that goes off to camp. *"I love you!"*

It might be a message on a sheet of paper in your child's binder. *"I'm praying for you today!"*

It might be a photo of a big fish that your child discovers in his tackle box as he goes on his first overnight fishing trip. *"I'm wishing you lots of luck!"*

Joanne recently told me about a habit her mother has had for the past twenty-five years. Her mother removes the stickers on fruit—bananas, melons, and the like—and immediately puts them someplace in her children's rooms, on their clothes, or among their possessions. All their growing up years, Joanne and her two brothers have found "Ripe" and "Chiquita Banana" stickers on the pages of their schoolbooks, on bedroom mirrors, on the labels of a favorite T-shirt or blouse, folded inside a washcloth in the bathroom, just about anyplace that's unexpected. The message conveyed was and is a simple one, "I'm thinking of you. I'm loving you even from afar."

Recently Joanne's brother phoned her from Central America to say, "You'll never guess what I found stuck on a packet of underwear as I was unpacking my suitcase after a visit to Mom's. That's right . . . a fruit sticker that said, 'Fresh!' "

Words of Encouragement   To a child, words of encouragement are synonymous with "I love you"—

> *"Way to go!"*
> *"I'm proud of you."*
> *"I believe in you."*
> *"I just know you can do it."*

Find a creative place to put that message. Choose a place where you are nearly one hundred percent sure your child will find it but will also be surprised to discover it. All of these phrases say to a child, "Mom and Dad believe in me. They love me enough to tell me so."

To a child, these are also messages that are readily understood as complimentary ways of saying, "Mom and Dad are behind me. They believe in me. They love me enough to stand with me." To your child, a sincere compliment or a word of thanks is also perceived as a message of love.

Scott reached into his fielder's mitt one day to pull out a message, "Mitt of a champion." It put a smile on his face and a calm in his heart as he headed out into right field for the first inning of the championship game.

"An American hero . . . a true trooper." That was the note left beside a plate with a couple of chocolate chip cookies when Terisa came home from a full day of picking up roadside litter with her Girl Scout troop.

One father rented a billboard-type sign and had it placed in front of the family home. "Home of the world's greatest third grader."

Another parent used his daughter's sidewalk chalk to write a giant message to his daughter on the driveway of their home.

Notes of Sincerity   Your notes don't need to be elaborate or expensive. They don't need to be daily. They don't need to be messages that anyone will see other than your child. They only need to be sincere. You can write them on a paper bag holding a granola bar that is stuffed inside a backpack, a crumpled up wad of notebook paper that's stuffed into the sleeve of a jacket, or a piece of masking tape that is taped to a basketball.

Make your expressions of love a surprise. Your child will know, "Mom loves me even when I'm out of her sight. Dad cares even when I'm not aware of it."

20 ✦ "Snap Out of It" or "Get Beyond It" Can Be Messages of Love

You will face a number of times in the course of raising your child in which "Snap out of it!" or "Get beyond it!" can be the greatest expression of concern and love you can show your child.

"Snap out of it" is another way of saying, "I love you too much to let you grow up to be a miserable person." You need to be on the alert for two types of behavior that can result in misery for your child down the line: whining and whimpering.

Whining A whining child is a miserable child to be around. Many adults overlook the fact that a child whines because he, too, is miserable.

What causes whining? Generally speaking, whining is caused by an unfulfilled expectation on the part of the child. The child wants something that he isn't being given. It may be attention, a toy, a second piece of candy, favor or acknowledgement from an adult, permission, a reward of some type—all of which boil down to the child's wish or will not being fulfilled or recognized.

Tell your child simply but firmly, "I refuse to allow you to grow up to be a miserable person. I will not accept whining. Not only will you not get what you want, but you will be sent to your room. I won't listen to this mournful sound. I want to see a happy face and, more importantly, a happy attitude. You can choose to be happy or content in this situation. You can choose to accept what you have and be grateful for it. You can choose to accept no for an answer."

If your child continues to whine, follow through. Send the child to his room or away from the rest of the group. Isolation stops whining faster than just about any other punishment. Go to your child later. If the whining starts again, leave your child alone or send him to his room a second time. In fact, leave your child alone until you get a positive answer to your question, "Are you ready to rejoin us with a happy heart?"

Whimpering There are many times when a child is truly hurt and she cries. She may have made a mistake or embarrassed herself in some way or been rejected or have experienced a bout of fear grounded in either an imaginary or real cause. Crying is an appropriate response for a child at such times, and the appropriate response from a parent is to hold the child and comfort her.

There are other times when a child whimpers because she simply isn't getting her way. She doesn't want to be left alone with the babysitter. She doesn't want to walk into her new classroom. She doesn't want big brother to reclaim his truck. Such cries are rooted in manipulation and ring false. Nearly every parent can tell in a second a real cry from a fake one.

Life holds many small challenges for a child, many unknowns and many risks. But a child will have the courage to face these challenges if he knows, "Mom thinks I can do this." Don't add to your child's doubts by displaying behavior that convinces your child he cannot handle the situation: "You're scared, so I'll stay."

Let your child know that life has tough moments but that you believe he can survive them. *"I know this may seem scary or hard for you to do, but I also know that you can do it. You have what it takes to make the most out of this hour without me. You have what it takes to turn a tough time into a terrific time."*

Love your child enough to insist that your child have a bright, positive attitude. "But that just isn't the personality of my child," you may say.

One of the most repeated phrases in the Bible is this: "Fear not. Rejoice!" Those words are stated as commands. Fear is not an acceptable behavior; joy is required. You have the privilege as a parent to say to your child, "Rejoice. And again I say, rejoice."

21 ✦ Give Your Child Heirloom Items

Give your child objects that say, "I love you so much that I want to give you this item that I treasure." What makes an item an heirloom? The fact that you like it and count it as a special item, or the fact that you have made it and, thus, it represents your time, effort, and skill.

What to Give   The item may be . . .

- a family photo album.
- a quilt.
- a painting.
- a family Bible.
- a rare book.
- a coin or stamp collection.
- a piece of furniture.
- a musical instrument.
- a watch.
- anything you value highly.

Such gifts convey to a child, "I'm glad you're part of this family. As a treasured child, you are worthy of family treasures."

When to Give It   When should you give heir-loom items to a child? When you are willing to let go of them and never ask about them again.

In many cases, especially with items easily broken or lost, you may want to let your child know, "This is going to be yours someday. It's my desire that you have it and that you will appreciate it so much that you will want to pass it along to someone you love as much as I love you." Mark the item with your child's name.

In some cases, you may want to keep an item on a high shelf or in a glass case for protection until such time as your child is old enough to take proper care of it. But once you have given an item you consider to be an heirloom to a child, don't ask about it, look for it, or even think about it. Consider it "passed along" and no longer yours. There's always a chance that your child won't value the item as much as you do. Don't let disappointment or resentment creep in. If you suspect that you are going to be hurt if the item is damaged, lost, or ignored, hold on to it until a later time or make it part of the estate you leave your child.

Giving heirloom items to your child sends two messages to your child. "I love you enough to give you this treasured item. And I expect you to live long, to prosper, and to extend the quality and char-acter of our family to another generation. Toward that end, I give you a family treasure." Both of those messages are laden with love.

22 ✦ Introduce Your Child

Don't let your child be invisible. Introduce him. Acknowledge her. Include your child wherever you are and with whomever you come into contact.

The child who is not introduced is a child who can easily conclude, "Dad's ashamed of me. Mom's forgotten me. I'm not worth much. They must love the attention of that person more than they value my feelings." It's not a very great leap for your child to feel unwanted and unloved.

Include Your Child Your child can learn something about you by being included in your conversations with other adults. He can discover that you are a valued member of another group, a work force or a club or a church group. He can discover that in your past, you were a lot like him.

If you need to discuss something privately with an adult you encounter, ask your child's permission for a few minutes alone with the person. "Sweetheart, I'm sure all this military talk is boring to you. If you'd like to go check out the Zingo ride, I'll meet you there in just a few minutes." Or, "Son, I need just a few seconds with Mrs. Jefferson to ask her a couple of questions. Would you mind taking these packages to the car?"

When you host a party, don't banish your children to an out-of-the-way corner. Introduce them to various guests. Let them sample the food you are serving. Let them enjoy a little of the party atmosphere. Then you can send them to bed or encourage them to go outside and play.

Teach Your Child   Teach your child:

- How to address adults. (Always give your child a clue. "This is Mrs. Jefferson." "This is Dr. Jones." Encourage your child to call adults by a title and last name.)
- How to shake hands. (Firmly.)
- How to handle compliments. (A simple thank you is generally sufficient.)
- How to interrupt graciously. ("Excuse me" instead of a tug on the sleeve.)

Including your child in adult conversations does two things for your child. First, it says to your child that you consider him worthy to be included and that you value his presence.

Second, it trains your child in important communication skills. It says to your child, "I want you always to be able to talk with anyone, anywhere. I want them to remember you when they meet you. You're worth remembering." A child who is included feels loved.

23 ✦ Have a Listening Ear

Listen to your child. It may sound overly simplistic, but the axiom is generally true: *listen to your child, and chances are, he'll listen to you.*

Clear Your Schedule Establish a time in your daily routine in which your child always knows that he can talk to you, whether he chooses to exercise that option or not. It may be while you are fixing dinner or in the quiet evening hours as you settle in for the night. It may be as soon as your child arrives home from school or in the car on the way to school.

Set apart time for being with your child. Make your time available to your child. (Make certain your child's calls can always get past a secretary or receptionist and through to you.)

Clear Your Mind *Clear your mind* so that you can truly "hear" what your child is telling you. Very often, the first thing that a child says to you is not what he ultimately wants to share with you. Learn to ask questions of your child without interrogating him. Ask, "How'd algebra go today?" instead of "Did you pass?"

Ask your child questions that can't be answered

with a simple yes or no. Ask, "What was the best thing that happened at school today?" instead of, "Did you have a good day at school?"

Help your child switch gears from his day's work. Help him unwind. Ask, "Hear any good jokes today?" instead of "How much homework do you have to do?"

Go into a listening time with a positive frame of mind. "I definitely sense something is about to be added to the prayer list. Care to share it?"

Clear Away the Clutter Turn off competing noises and chatter. Turn off the television set or the car radio. A segue may be helpful in establishing a listening mood.

- Provide an afternoon snack and sit down with your child to enjoy it with him.
- Read with your child for a few minutes. That's often a time when your child will be willing to exchange a few more words with you.
- Sit on the edge of the bed with your child for a few minutes after—or before—bedtime prayers.

A child who knows you have a listening ear is a child who knows you have a loving heart.

24 ✦ Send a Card

Give your child the excitement and fun of receiving a card in the mailbox addressed just to him! Have you ever noticed that adults seem to get all the mail? From a child's perspective, "getting mail" is an adult activity, including sorting the mail, opening it, and discarding it. When a child receives a piece of mail all his own, addressed specifically to him at his own home, he not only receives a wonderful treat, but as part of the very process, an important threefold message.

- You are an important part of this world, as important as any adult. Adult systems can also be enjoyed and employed by children. A part of growing up is learning how and when to use these systems.
- You have a place at this address, in this home.
- You have total control over the mail you receive. It is your privilege to open it, keep it or throw it away, read it or not, and respond or not.

Cards are a graphic way of underscoring what you say to your child orally. Children can hold a card. By touching it and "possessing" it, they experience its message in a way that is different from hearing the spoken word. Children can reread a card . . . and reread it. Children are concrete thinkers. They often believe a written message more than a verbal one simply because it is something they can see and touch.

Young children will often carry their cards until they are tattered and well splattered. "Mine," they say. My card, my mom and dad (or aunt, uncle, grandparent, godparent, or other friend)—my loving relationship.

Cards are also a great way for parents who travel a great deal to send a message of love to their children.

Rene's father is a truck driver. He sends her cards that she sometimes receives even after her father has returned home from a run. They are important to her, nevertheless, as an expression that even though her father is away a great deal of the time, he carries her in his heart.

Remember your children, too, as you send greeting cards at traditional times. Eight-year-old Kay Ellen has a scrapbook with nothing but birthday cards and birthday party photos in it. She has cards for each birthday from her aunt, both sets of her grandparents, and her parents, even cards for her first two birthdays, which she doesn't remember.

Cards are a good way for you to communicate with a child who is away at camp or visiting a relative. Try sending a humorous card. Will's mother did, with an added note, "I thought you might need a laugh about now." Little did she know that the card would arrive the same day that her son broke out with poison ivy welts.

Finally, cards are a way for your child to show others that you care. They are subtle but important evidence: "My Mommy sent me this. My Mommy loves me." Feeling your love is critically important to your child. It is also important for your child to be able to declare the fact of your love to others.

You should also feel free to make your own cards. Have a cut and paste session with your child periodically. Let her cut the illustrations from cards that have previously been sent to you and turn them into new cards. Then, turn right around and send one of those cards to your child with a message of love and appreciation. "Thanks, honey, for helping us save a tree." Or, "I couldn't have done it without you!"

- Cards are inexpensive.
- They take relatively little time to choose and send.
- They offer you a "platform" of thoughts to which you may add other lines that you find difficult to say in a face-to-face encounter.

All in all, cards are a great way to say "I love you" to a child.

25 ✦ Project the Fact of Your Love into the Future

Share a vision with your child for what you hope your child's life will be like in the future, even for all eternity. Include your love and a loving relationship with your child as part of that vision. Let your child know that you expect your love for him to last forever.

This does *not* mean that you should tell your child what you expect him to do in his future or what he should choose as a career. Insist that your child prepare for his future by acquiring certain skills, from learning to make his own bed to staying in school). But mostly, take delight in your child as she discovers her own potential and makes decisions about her own career path.

What you *can* say to your child are statements such as these:

- *"I can hardly wait to see what our lives are like fifty years from now. You'll probably be telling me to buckle my seatbelt on the way to the grocery store, just as I am telling you now. What kind of car do you suppose we'll be riding in?"*
- *"I look forward to the day when you'll invite me to your house for dinner. I hope we can laugh and*

have a good time in your kitchen, just like we do now. I wonder what you'll fix? What do you think, hot dogs or hamburgers?"

- *"I'm going to miss you when you go off to college. Life will have fewer surprises, such as discovering what is stuffed under your bed. Life will also be a lot quieter. I'm not sure I'll be able to handle the opportunity to use the phone whenever I want! It's going to be fun, though, to see what major you choose."*

Weave your projections of a future loving relationship into the casual course of daily life. Let your child begin to imagine the close parent-child relationship you will have in the future. Let him know that you expect to be a part of his life always as a loving supportive person.

This does *not* mean you should convey that you expect to live with your child or that you have a desire for your child always to be dependent upon you. Quite the contrary. Establish an expectation that your child will one day be an independent adult and that you look forward to communicating and relating to him as such. Establish an expectation that although the nature of your relationship may change, the love between you will never be diminished.

- After a conversation with your child on a serious topic or a conversation in which you have shared hard-to-express emotions, you may want to say in conclusion, "I hope we can always have

good conversations like this. I hope you always feel that you can talk to me."
- After a joking, playful, fun time, let your child know, "I can't imagine not being able to laugh with you for the next hundred thousand million years!"
- After a time of punishment, hug your child and assure him, "You know something? Someday you're going to be too big for me to spank, but you're never going to be too big for me to hug!"

Let your child know, too, that you believe in his ability to be a moral, law-abiding citizen. Letting your child know that you believe in his bright side, his ability to do good, and in his opportunities for success is another way of saying, "I love you and from the vantage point of my love, I can see wonderful attributes within you."

Love means hoping for your child's best success, believing in your child's best nature, and looking forward to your child's best gifts to the world. Share this loving vision with your child. It is a way of conveying, "My love for you will never end."

26 ✦ Encourage and Establish Private Jokes

Share enough experiences with your child and you will end up with a bucketful of private jokes—fun, playful, just-you-two memories that your child will cherish all his life. Your child will know that "Dad and I have a good time when we're together. Mom and I laugh a lot. We're on the same wavelength. Our hearts are beating in tune."

My grandfather had a wonderful ability to distill his love into a wink (accompanied by just the hint of a smile). No matter what Grandma was saying or Mom was doing, no matter where we were or what the circumstances, Grandpa could send a large dose of love straight from his heart to mine in a fleeting instant. I was always surprised when he turned to me and winked. I was always pleased.

What makes for a private joke? A moment of teasing that you both enjoy, a shared sense of what is humorous in the world, an ability to laugh at the human condition.

Teasing isn't fun if the one being teased doesn't think so. Then teasing is perceived as harrassment. (Siblings know this far more readily than parents sometimes.)

Some Guidelines   Be sure you observe some simple guidelines for teasing:

- Tease your child only if you are willing to be teased back.
- Even as you tease, respect your child. Don't tease about his mistakes, his accomplishments, or about any behavior that you or your child are trying to change (or which you think should be changed). In other words, don't tease a child about anything over which he is perceived to have some degree of control. Tease him about the funny tie he chooses to wear but not about his weight or his stammering.
- Never tease a child in front of his friends or strangers.
- Tease primarily in the context of imaginary situations. ("We're in big trouble if we ever take Gabbie to the zoo. Imagine an elephant coming over to greet him the way his dog just did!")
- Tease always with love, never as a method of teaching or as a punishment.

Encourage Laughter   Let your child know that laughter is a wonderful commodity in our world. Laugh aloud at the movie you attend with your child. Laugh aloud at the circus clown. Laugh aloud at cartoons you watch with your child.

I've never met a young child who didn't find a certain amount of humor in physical comedy, the pie-in-the-face slapstick variety. Adults often try to stifle their amusement at those types of comedic situations because they don't want to encourage such behavior in their children. Go ahead and laugh! Let your child know it's OK to laugh at performers who are doing a show in which slapstick humor is included. Point out that the people in the show aren't really injured but that it is *never* appropriate to laugh at someone who truly is injured or sick.

Never laugh at your child. Teach him to laugh at himself. How? By laughing at your own self!

Make light of what might seem like embarrassing moments. Don't overemphasize them, ignore them, or be chagrined by them.

If you can laugh at yourself, and your child sees that you can, your child will learn to laugh at himself. He will find pleasure in human differences and in the little accidents of life.

Laughing with your child in this manner conveys an important message to your child: "My love is not contingent on your perfection. You are a human being. So am I. The love between us transcends our human foibles."

27 ✦ Apologize When You Need To

Let your child know that you make mistakes, that you aren't the perfect parent. Admit your mistakes. Confess them. Let your child know you will most likely make mistakes in the future, even though you don't want to make them.

Admit Your Mistakes Perfection is a terrible burden for both you and your child. I have yet to meet a child who didn't forgive and who didn't respond with love to a parent who admitted a mistake. That's good news! Accepted apologies bring healing to your child and to your relationship. Hearing and accepting your apologies allows your child to let go of feelings of resentment before they can fester into bitterness.

By admitting your own mistakes and letting your child hear that your love transcends your mistakes, you are also giving your child the confidence that comes through knowing that no mistake, error, goof, flub, or accident that *he* commits can destroy the love you feel for him.

Establish again and again that your love is not based on perfect behavior, either yours or your child's. Love transcends behavior.

I've never believed the line from the movie *Love Story* in which the heroine says to her beloved, "Love means never having to say you're sorry." In my opinion, love means that you are *always* willing to say you're sorry when you have done something that has caused hurt to another person.

Pick the Right Time When should you apologize?

- In a private moment. Don't grandstand; your child will find your apology to be insincere. You may need to apologize publicly if the mistake you have made is a public one that included people other than your child. In those cases, apologize to your child first. Let him know that you are *most* sorry that he was hurt by your behavior.
- Never apologize unless you are truly sorry for the thing you have done. Some people apologize solely to smooth over a tense situation or to appease someone else, while, in their heart of hearts, they aren't the least bit repentant.
- Only apologize to the extent that you feel regret. You may have *no* regret for punishing your child for his knocking over the entire cookie display in a willful act of anger-filled disobedience at the supermarket. You may, however, be sorry that you spanked your child right there in the supermarket aisle. Apologize, in that case,

for the way in which you punished your child, not for the fact that you did.

• If your child was hurt as the result of an accident on your part, apologize for the fact of the accident. Assure your child that it was an accident, not a willful act on your part. (Your child probably already knows this, but it doesn't hurt for you to say so.) Don't self-justify. Apologize for being the source of pain.

• Don't bother with an apology if you have no intention of changing your future behavior so as *not* to make the same mistake again. It is a hollow apology to say, "I'm sorry I hit you last night" as a consequence of having had too much alcohol—unless you stop drinking (and seek the help that may be necessary to enable you to stop).

• Don't try to cover up your own bad behavior with an apology. Don't assume that just because you apologize each time you are late picking your daughter up at her dance class that you can continue to be late. Your child will eventually know that your apology is just so many empty words.

Your apologies, in sum, must be genuine, heartfelt, and bear the fruit of changed behavior. If they don't, they will be perceived by your child as lies. How, then, can your child trust you when you say "I love you?"

28 ✦ Have a Special Whistle Just for Your Child

I can't duplicate the whistle that my father has used to get my attention ever since I was born. I just can't seem to make the sound he does, even though I have tried repeatedly.

Recently my father and I became separated as we were shopping in a large department store. I continued to browse through the racks of clothing, unaware that he had gone in another direction and had lost sight of me. Suddenly, I heard that familiar "daddy call." I found him in a matter of seconds, much to the surprise of the clerk standing next to him.

"But," she sputtered, "how did you hear him? Nobody else paid any attention."

"I come when he calls," I said with a laugh. "Just like a well-conditioned puppy!"

A Reward Although I was attempting to be humorous, in actuality, Daddy's whistle *has* had some conditioning associated with it. I have always been rewarded for responding by being in my father's presence. His whistle is associated with being safe, protected, found, related, loved.

Ultimately, the message has always been the

same. "Daddy loves me enough to find me. He wants my attention. He wants me to be with him. He wants me to see him or hear him."

A Warning   I am fairly certain my brother has a little different feeling about Daddy's whistle. He has generally heard it at times when he was doing something that he shouldn't have been doing. To him, the whistle is a call to "get out of the trouble you're about to get yourself into."

A Call to Attention   I was surprised one day to hear my friend Ellie call her children. She used a different whistle, one unique to her family. "It comes in handy," she said, "when you have two explorers for children. They follow their noses faster than my feet can move." What does Ellie's whistle convey to her children? The same message: "Mommy loves us enough to find us. She wants us to be with her."

A love whistle gives your child confidence that "Daddy knows how to get in touch with me if we lose touch. He loves me and doesn't want to lose me. Mommy cares enough about me to get my attention when I'm about to make a mistake. She loves me and doesn't want me to get in trouble."

29 ✦ Take Time to Play with Your Child

Have a playtime with your child every day. Let your child know that you like his world, and that you want to have fun with him doing the things that he likes to do.

A few years ago, I encountered a boy named Bert. Bert was a real brat, always creating trouble, always looking for a way out of trouble, always justifying the trouble he caused.

Something wonderful happened to Bert, however. His father put down his newspaper and turned off the TV and started playing games with his son. Dad spotted a real ability in Bert to think ahead and to manipulate. He channeled that ability into a few chess lessons.

In themselves, the chess games didn't generate a lot of conversation, but they did create a bond. Bert felt less and less need to get his father's attention.

Dad also applied some of the rules of chess to other areas of life. ("The Queen is the player that is the most valuable because she can move in all directions. Life's like that. You want to be able to move in all directions. You need an education to do that.") Bert listened.

Learning Through Play   Bert learned to play by the rules, in life as well as the game of chess. He learned how to call on the advice and help of others. He learned how to compete; how to win and lose. The truths encountered in the example of Bert and his father can be applied to nearly all game-playing activity between parents and their children.

- Through playtime, your child acquires an ever-growing awareness that you are available to him.
- Through playtime, your child learns how to play.
- Through playtime, your child finds a relaxed environment for communicating with you.
- Through playtime, your child learns that skills can be improved.
- Through playtime, your child learns how *you* play.

Who Makes the Rules?

Within the bounds of safety and morality, let your child set the rules and limits. *"You take the white piece, I'll take the red one."* Let your child dictate the pace of the play and govern the match.

If you must make suggestions, do so only to trigger imagination. Don't force your ideas.

Play with your child. He will have your time. He will have your attention. He will have numerous opportunities for learning, growing, sharing. In that, he will feel your love.

30 ✦ Give Equal Attention to Each Child

One of the Smothers Brothers' famous comedy routines is based on the principle, "Mom loved you best." We laugh, in part, because we recognize or have experienced the truth underlying the jest.

Be Fair to Each Child Did you take eighteen hours of videotape of your firstborn, only to forget to pull out the camcorder once your second or third child arrived? Do you have an album full of photos of your firstborn and only a smattering of snapshots of your other children?

Does your daughter have claim to all the family linens, quilts, and other heirloom needlepoint? What about your son?

Are you making plans to help your son buy a car when he turns sixteen? Do you talk about helping your daughter in the same way?

- Your child needs to know that he or she has *equal access to your time and attention.* Each child needs to know, "Mom has time just for *me.*" This is especially true when a new baby arrives in a family and the older child or children tend to get lost in the shuffle.

- Your child needs *equal access to your applause.* Each child needs to be able to count on her parents to be present for her performances, with loud applause and the heart of a fan.
- Your child needs *equal access to your display of pride.* The disparaging difference in photo albums is an example of unequal display of pride. In this instance, the problem could be remedied simply by sitting down at the beginning of each new year and scheduling two or three "photo shoot" days on your family calendar.
- Your child needs *equal access to your gifts.* Older children and favored children tend to get more of "the good stuff." Money flows more freely when there is one child instead of five.
- Your child needs *equal access to an inheritance.* No matter the reasons that may be cited, no child ever understands an unequal dividing of family property or heirloom treasures.

Each Child Is Unique Each child's personality is different. Sometimes you will find that you understand one child better than another or that you empathize with one child more than another or that your personality meshes better with one child more than another. Those differences are normal and to be expected. Your child probably enjoys being with one parent more than the other in certain circumstances.

Don't let these differences, however, influence your love. You do have enough love for each child.

31 ✦ Take Your Child with You

Just as you find time to play with your child, give your child an opportunity to enter into your world. This, too, conveys the message, "I love you and enjoy being with you!"

In early November, my father often allowed me to ride with him during his evening trips to take loaded cotton trailers to the gin. I still remember those times of togetherness, of braving the dark unknown, accomplishing an important task, and greeting the gin clerks as if I were a "big girl." It seemed special to be allowed to go out at night; it must have been all of 6:30 P.M.!

In the Workplace John takes his children to the office on Saturday mornings when he goes in to catch up on the week's mail. The children sit in the conference room adjacent to his office and have a task of their own to complete during the hour or two they are in the office: a set of new crayola pictures for the bulletin board that hangs on the back of John's door.

Occasionally John will call his children on the phone that connects the two rooms, just to see if there is anything they need. They know their way down to the office cafeteria, and at least once during the morning, they all head for the coffee and hot chocolate vending machines. Mostly, they work, and he works.

John's children have a good idea where Daddy is when he isn't at home, what their Daddy does during the day, and how their daddy feels about work. At the end of their mutual work session, the children hang up their drawings, and they all make the rounds through the office in order that John might leave messages on various desks and check to make certain that various machines have been left on or turned off.

Running Errands   Andrea takes her daughters with her every time she goes to the beauty shop to have her hair cut, frosted, or permed. Sometimes her two daughters have their hair cut. Most of the time, they sit and read the books they have brought along, watch the various procedures, and choose styles from books provided by the shop. Once, Andrea treated them to a manicure.

Over the years, the girls have learned a lot by watching people come and go. They have learned that everybody likes a different style, that it takes organizational ability to do just about any task in life, and that it is important to be able to communicate exactly how short you want your bangs cut! They are experiencing a part of their mother's world. They know that Mom enjoys their company and wants them to share her life.

32 ✦ Honor Your Child's Privacy

Don't snoop through his things. Don't read her diary. Don't monitor his phone calls. Don't rummage through her special box of treasures.

Honor your child's right to privacy. That sends a message to your child: "I love you enough to trust you. There's nothing you can do or hide that will destroy my love for you. At the same time, I don't need to know everything you say or do. My love is not rooted in your behavior, but in who you are as my child. I love you enough to let you become independent, but I also love you enough to insist that you never become alienated."

Very often, family arguments over privacy stem from a lack of initial, clear definitions as to what may be considered private and what may not be.

A Parent's Requirements Your child's room is not only your *child's* room. It is a room in *your* house. You can require that it be kept clean (with neatness negotiable), that no structural damage be done (such as a hole in the wall), and no structural changes be made without your permission (including curtains pulled from their rods), that certain limitations may be placed on decor (no nude posters, perhaps), and that certain items may not be kept in it (snakes, for example).

Let your child know that you plan to clean his room periodically. (The alternative, of course, is for your child to do the cleaning and to do a thorough job of it.)

Tell your child you retain the right to enter her room any time you smell smoke. Let your child know that if she has friends over and chooses to entertain them in her room, that you consider her room to have then taken on the nature of a public meeting place and that you retain the right to enter at any time, although you will knock first and not stay. You may require that the door be left open if your teenager entertains someone of the opposite sex.

A Child's Privilege You can—and should—designate certain areas within your child's room as "private." Your child's diary is private. So is a box for keeping letters. The top drawer of your child's desk may be a place for private things. You may even want to give your child a box, desk, or locker space that can be locked. (Make sure you have a spare key somewhere so you can gain access should your child lose his key.) Your child's conversations with his friends are private.

However, you have the privilege of determining what is allowed inside your home. That includes what books and magazines may be kept in your home, what programs may be watched or listened to (in your child's room, too, not only on the main set downstairs), what music is aired, what games can be played, and who and what may be allowed access into your home (four-legged, two-legged, and no-legged creatures!)

By establishing the limits of your child's privacy, you are also extending the freedoms of it. Your child can have the assurance that his phone calls will not be monitored, that his correspondence will not be censored, that his conversations and activities with his friends will not be spied upon, and above all, that you desire for him to be a responsible person who will make responsible choices.

You may make errors in setting the boundaries of privacy or in allowing certain items into your home. You must never err, however, in retaining the right to determine the limits of privacy.

You are also conveying three of the most important "tough love" lessons your child needs to learn under your roof:

- Love is a means for getting along in a society—in a family, in a community, in a group. It is not a license for doing anything you want to do or for alienating yourself from a group norm.
- Love does not free us to do evil. Love constrains us from doing evil.
- Love is the motive for extending, sharing, and promoting life—not limiting it, harming it, or destroying it.

33 ✦ Have a "Date" with Your Child

Make being with your child an active choice, not a consequence: "I'll be with my child if there's nothing else to do." Choose to be with your child.

Let your child hear you say to someone that he knows you enjoy being with: "Oh, I'd like to go with you, but I have a prior date with my child."

Plan a Date with Your Child. Spend an entire evening with your child. Choose to do it and count it as important, as important as you considered your first date with your spouse.

On your date, talk about what your child wants to talk about. That may mean a conversation devoted totally to the antics of the hottest TV character, the latest fad, or the current second-grader jokes. Eat what your child likes to eat. Go to his or her favorite restaurant. Be prepared for burgers or pizza.

From the time Melody was ten until she was eighteen, she had a date with her father on the second Friday night of every month ending in a *y* or an *r*—January, February, May, July, September, October, November, December.

Your date with your child need not be elaborate or

expensive. It need only be a date that you set, keep, and enjoy.

Make an Appointment with Your Child.
Put it on your work calendar. Two o'clock on the first Thursday afternoon of the month. That was the set appointment time that Stell had with her daughter, Gracie. Stell gave Gracie a note to give to her teacher on Monday of the designated week and a second reminder note on Thursday morning.

Stell cleared her work schedule, allowing nothing to interfere. She had the "Thursday time" preestablished with her boss as a condition of her employment and worked through the lunch hour on Monday, Tuesday, and Wednesday of the first week of the month. On Thursdays, she left her office promptly at 1:30 P.M. and took a cab to pick up Gracie.

Once they were both in the cab, Stell and Gracie would change gears. Down came Stell's hair and off came her jewelry. She would pull casual shoes from her briefcase to replace her heels. They would stop by their apartment just long enough to dump their things and get right back into the same cab to head for the zoo, the park, the amusement park, or a late matinee movie. Just the two of them. They would have dinner out, maybe just a deli sandwich.

Once a month during the school year. Nine appointments a year for five years running. A total of forty-five, three-hour "appointments." A lifetime of happy memories.

34 ✦ Display Your Child's Photograph

Put your child on display—at least in a photographic format. Let your child see, in a tangible way, that you are proud of him and desire for others to know that he or she is your child. Send a message to your child: "I'm glad to be associated with you in the eyes of the world."

- *Have a photo of your child at your place of work— if that is appropriate*—on a desk, credenza, bookshelf. That way, when your child comes to see you in your place of employment, he will have the message reinforced: "My mother is thinking about me even when she can't be at home with me."
- *Carry your child's photograph in your wallet or purse.* My own father's wallet is about three inches thick. Why? Because he still carries at least a dozen of his favorite photographs of my brother and me. Every child loves to rummage through a daddy's wallet or a mommy's purse. Let them find themselves in the process.
- *Take photographs of your child with you as you travel.* Let your child see you packing his or her

framed photograph into your suitcase. The message? "Daddy is taking me along in his heart."

* *Have photographs of your child on display in your own home.* Give visitors the opportunity to admire them and your child the opportunity to see himself in the context of his own home. Especially have photographs in areas that you consider your private space—boudoir, bedroom, home office.

Include photos that show your child in action. Don't limit yourself to school pictures. Include photos that show you with your child. Include photos that remind you of special moments shared with your child, moments in which your child is discovering the world, moments in which your child displays spontaneous joy.

When displaying family photos in a grouping, include photos of yourself and your spouse as a child, as well as photos of grandparents and other family members. Let your child see himself as a valuable and welcome part of the whole clan. Express to your child the message of continuity, "You are an important member of our family. We all love you, just as we have loved one another down through the years."

Consider having a formal portrait taken of your child at least once or twice during his growing-up years.

Photographs say to your child, "Any scene is better with you in it." And that's an expression of love!

35 ✦ Require the Truth

Do not accept lies from your child—ever. Insist upon honesty. Do not let a pattern develop in which your child believes, "Mom (or Dad) has a tolerance for lies." Such a belief leads a child to conclude that "it's possible Mom and Dad are lying when they tell me they love me."

Speak the truth to your child. Continually pull your child back to reality and to an accountability for the truth. Children have an inborn capacity for imagination and for fantasy. Much of the growing-up experience for a child is actually a ferreting out of fact from fiction. It is the parent's role to continually call a child back from fantasy to face the real world.

This does *not* mean that you should avoid any activities that promote your child's ability to imagine. On the contrary, the development of your child's imagination is an important aspect of developing his creativity and his expressive potential. It *does* mean that you refuse to let your child dwell perpetually in a fantasy world.

Fact versus Fiction Talk with your child about the reality of television programs. Ask, "What was real in that story and what wasn't?" Ask, "Do you think people like that really exist?" Ask, "Why wouldn't that be a likely story in real life?" Help your child distinguish between fiction and documentary.

Little White Lies Some parents find "little white lies" acceptable, even cute. Don't be among them. The telling of any lie instills a belief in a child that lying is not only acceptable but sometimes it is preferable and, occasionally, even fun. Lying becomes, all too easily, a means for manipulation of others.

The number-one hearer of your child's lie is not you, it is your child. A child hears himself lie and, in some small way, accepts his own lie as being true. Lies and truth thus become confused. A child who falls into the habit of telling lies eventually doesn't know *how* to tell the truth—to himself or to others— and may not even recognize the truth.

Keep your child's feet planted firmly in reality and let him take an occasional break to escape into an imaginary world with imaginary friends, a world in which he, no doubt, will be the hero or the star. Don't let your child live in a fantasy world, taking only an occasional reality break for brushing his teeth or tying his shoelaces.

Practice Telling Details

- Ask your child to tell about an incident that really happened. You might say, "Darling, you tell the story about seeing the lions at Safari

Land." Encourage details. *"How many lions were there? What did they do? What did they look like? What was said by those of us in the car?"*

- Ask your child to play journalist. Point out to your child the necessity for details, the importance of facts, the descriptive power of elaboration. *"What did he say? What did she say? When? How? Where? Who? What was the result? Why do you think this happened?"*
- Ask your child to tell you about a book she has finished. *"What was the plot? What were the characters like? Where was the story set?"*

Such activities give your child practice in speaking the truth, in developing rationales, and in prioritizing information.

Finally, a child who is allowed to lie and get away with it begins to develop an assumption that all people lie and get away with it.

Love is based on trust. It is also based on truth. When you say to your child, "I love you," you want your child to believe you and to *know* that you are telling him or her the rock-bottom, no-frills truth. Allowing a pattern of lies to develop in your child's life clouds the capacity of your child to hear the truth of your love.

36 ✦ Give Your Child a Party

Every child loves to be the center of attention, even the child who seems the most shy or reserved. Nothing puts a child on center stage more than a party in his or her honor. Give your child

- a birthday party,
- a reception after confirmation or first communion or baptism,
- a graduation party (from any grade or course of study you choose).

Or just invite your child's friends over for an afternoon or evening of fun—a swim party, barbecue, costume party, or a Valentine dance.

There's nothing in the rule book of life that says you can't give your child a surprise party on any day of the year. It doesn't need to be in commemoration of a birthday.

If it is not a surprise party, let your child be the host or hostess of the party. Rehearse with your child in advance how to be a host, greet people, mingle among the guests, serve refreshments, make introductions, and bid guests good-bye at the door.

A Mother-Daughter Social Early one autumn, Stacey invited five of her daughter's friends to a no-gifts, fancy-dress tea party. The moms were included in the invitation. The mothers dressed up and so did their daughters. Tables were set with lace and china. Mums were cut from the garden.

Shelley, Stacey's daughter, greeted all her friends at the door with a single flower, which the little girls then put into a vase to make a centerpiece bouquet. She showed each of her friends her placecard at the table.

While the little girls sipped punch and ate cookies and petit fours, the mothers sipped tea and coffee, ate finger sandwiches and lemon tarts, and watched their daughters through the slats of the louvered doors that separated their tea party from the one their daughters were enjoying.

As the afternoon drew to a conclusion, Stacey took a portrait-style photo of each girl and her mother out in their garden. (A few weeks later, guess what Stacey gave to her friends as Christmas presents?) Shelley loved being a hostess. Today, nearly twenty years later, she has her own catering and party-planning business.

Memories of Love A party gives your child a wonderful opportunity to be the center of attention, to receive the thanks, congratulations, or kind words of friends or relatives. A party gives your child a memory that will last a lifetime.

37 ✦ Lend Your Moral Support in Times of Crisis or Challenge

Every parent walks a fine line between mothering and smothering, between being a hand-holding daddy and a hands-off father. Your child needs your moral support in two types of circumstances: when he is experiencing something or someone for the first time, and when he is feeling more fear than faith.

Learn to recognize these times. Be sensitive to them, and be there for your child. He will always remember your presence and support as a living example of your love.

Be there with encouragement and support when your child

- Has his or her first haircut.
- Goes to the doctor or dentist.
- Enters a new school or a new grade.
- Meets a new babysitter.
- Has his first stage performance.
- Leaves for her first date.

Identify those occasions when your child is facing a new routine, learning a new skill, or meeting a new group of people. *Be* there at those critical times.

Ways to Show Support

- Tell your child as much as you can about what to expect. Explain how to make friends, how to ask getting-acquainted questions, what the rules are. Give your child as much advance preparation as possible. If your child is facing a performance, give him an opportunity for a dress rehearsal at home.
- Go with your child. Don't drop your child off at curbside. Go into the classroom, through the backstage doors, into the examining room.
- Help your child break the ice. Point out the familiar. Explain the unfamiliar. Make a few introductions or ask a few names.
- Give your child a parting show of encouragement—a thumbs-up sign, a wave, a blown kiss, a shoulder hug, a wink. Don't embarrass your child by staying around too long. At the same time, don't allow your child to cling to you. Let your child go to his seat in the class or on the team bench. Wait for a conversation to begin or for the adult in charge to take over. Disappear quietly and discreetly.
- Let your child know before you leave when you will be back and where you will be in the interim. Leave a phone number if you're going to

be somewhere other than home or work. Make sure your child knows when and where he is going to be with you again.

It is a real mark of maturity for a child to reach the place where he says about a first encounter, "It's OK, you don't need to go in with me." When that happens, be pleased! Smile and say, "OK!"

A child who is habitually left alone to face new challenges may grow up to be tough, but he is also likely to have a less tender heart. Don't let your child come to the conclusion, "Mom says she loves me, but she abandons me just when I need her the most. Dad says he loves me, but he's never there when I need the security of his presence."

Love means being available to your child when your child needs you. Say "I love you" with your very presence.

38 ✦ Allow Your Child to Choose a Treat

From time to time, let your child choose a treat for no reason other than she is your child. Reinforce the overriding fact of your love, "I love you just because you are my son, my daughter!"

Occasional Surprises Kelley lets her children create a kid's menu occasionally. She allows each of her four children to choose one food for the evening meal. (It can't be a dessert.) One recent meal combined steamed rice with butter, hot dogs (and buns), deviled eggs, and clam chowder. Another meal combined fish sticks, ravioli, applesauce, and peanut butter and jelly sandwiches.

About once a month, Sue will say to her daughter, "Why don't you choose something from the cosmetic counter while I do the grocery shopping? Top limit of six dollars!" Kristine has a great time deciding among the lipsticks, nail polishes, and other makeup items. At other times, Sue will give her the option of choosing any magazine she wants from the fairly extensive selection available in the same store. Kristine is learning to make choices and is receiving treats at the same time.

Surprise your child with an unexpected treat. Here are some examples.

- *"Why don't you pick out a package of cookies for us?"*
- *"Here's five dollars. I'm going to stay in the car while you run into the bakery and pick out two of your favorite donuts. Bring me one you think I'd like, too."*
- *"Let's each get a new CD. I reserve the right to approve the lyrics, though."*
- *"Let's stop and get an ice cream cone. Choose any flavor you want—one scoop or two!"*
- *"Here's ten dollars to spend on anything you like at the amusement park. If the item costs more than that, you'll have to use your own allowance money. If you don't want to buy anything, that's fine, too."*
- *"Let's stop here at this store on our way out so you can pick out a new bow for your hair. You decide."*

Reasonable Limits   At other times, insist that your child not beg, whine, or ask repeatedly for treats. Assure your child that you will provide for his or her basic needs. Remind your child that he can always use his allowance money or earnings for some items. Let treats be at your initiative.

Insist that your child not go beyond the treat you designate. Define the treat clearly and stick with your definition. Not two hair bows—one. Not fifteen dollars—ten dollars. Not an ice cream sundae—a cone, with a two-scoop maximum.

Don't link your treats with a behavior. Let your child pick out a package of cookies or an album independent of a victory or loss in his life. Let your child be surprised with a treat that is totally unrelated to his performance or accomplishments.

Suggest treats that your child might think are for a slightly "older kid." Let your eleven-year-old choose a lipstick, with the clear stipulation that she can't wear lipstick in public and that this is only for practice before the mirror in her room. Let your twelve-year-old son pick out an after-shave to be used only on those occasions when he is wearing a suit. Your child will be surprised at your level of confidence in him.

Let the treat be enjoyed primarily by your child. Give your child the first cookie out of the package, the first piece of pie. Treats say to your child, "Mom and Dad think I'm special just for who I am." That's love!

39 ✦ Share a Song with Your Child

Celebrate the relationship you have with your child in song. Many lovers have a song they refer to as "our song," usually a song that evokes memories of an important time together—a first date, a first dance together, an engagement night. You and your child have a loving relationship, too, and a song can help remind your child of happy moments spent with you.

- *"Your song" may be a tune that you hear together on a joyful occasion.* Perhaps it is one you hear on the radio as you make your way to a favorite picnic ground, a song that's playing on your stereo one night when a giggly mood hits and you enjoy a wild 'n' crazy time washing dishes, a song that gets stuck on a mall loudspeaker as you are in the final rush of Christmas shopping. "Your song" can be whatever song you remember as the song related to an enjoyable moment you have shared.

- *"Your song" may be a piece of music that is played frequently in your home.* Peter grew up in a home in which both parents had a deep love for classical music. The music of Johannes Brahms was frequently playing on his parent's stereo.

Today, nearly fifteen years later, those symphonies still evoke for Peter a remembrance of his parent's cozy living room and quiet evenings spent working jigsaw puzzles with his father as his mother sat nearby working on a needlepoint project.

For Dorena, the music was jazz. Her father loved to listen to the early albums, and he had a number of 78s that he played on the family hi-fi console. When Dorena is feeling a little homesick these days, she goes to the listening section of the library near her dormitory and plays "memories of home." Dad and Mom seem a little closer.

- *"Your song" may be a song that you make up especially for your child.* You don't need to be a composer or lyricist to come up with a song that you sing just for your child. Pick a tune that is familiar to you or make up a tune, and sing whatever words come to mind. Make it a love song. Keep it simple. Use your child's name as part of the lyrics.

I made up a song for three of my godchildren who are all in the same family. I let them know early on that this song was just for them and that I didn't sing it to anyone else. The words are exceedingly simple: "Who loves Kurtie? I love Kurtie. Who loves Kurtie? I'm the one who does!" The same song works equally well for sisters Katelyn and Kiersten. The phrase "I'm the one who does" is accompanied by tickles. You are welcome to use it with your child.

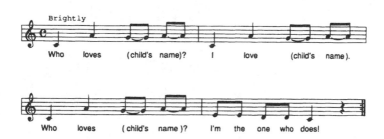

- *"Your song" may be a hymn.* It might be a rousing rendition of *"Onward Christian Soldiers"* that you sing together while you're fixing sack lunches or *"Amazing Grace"* sung together occasionally as a family bedtime song or *"My Faith Looks Up to Thee"* sung to your child in cozy times of comfort. Choose a hymn that both you and your child enjoy. Learn all the verses, and sing it with gusto.

Don't be surprised if you hear your child singing "your song" to himself as he plays quietly or prepares himself for facing a new challenge. That's the value of having a mutually loved song—your child can sing it to evoke memories of your strength, courage, presence, and zest for living at any time and in virtually any place without calling too much attention to himself. Let a song encapsulate your love. Sing or play it often.

40 ✦ Be Willing to Share Your Child with Other Adults

Don't set yourself up to be the only source of love your child experiences. Your child may not recognize the difference now, but he will feel cheated later. Share your child with other adults who love him. Let him know the joy of being loved by all of his grandparents, aunts and uncles, godparents, and other adults with whom he may have a bond.

The love from other adults serves as a reinforcement of your love. Their words of love back up your expressions of love and give your words, "I love you," even greater meaning. Their love brings your child to the conclusion that he is, indeed, lovable— not just by a parent who is often perceived as "having" to love the child, but by others who don't "have" to.

Often, parents knowingly, and sometimes unknowingly, attempt to shield their child from others because they, themselves, have been hurt. This is especially true in the case of divorce or separation. As hurt as you may have been, strive to see the world through your child's eyes. Your child will feel punished by you if he is denied access to those he has grown to love.

Valued Companions How can you tell which adults your child should have as regular companions? Let him be around those adults who value his presence and who enjoy being with him. Don't force your child on an unwilling grandparent. At the same time, recognize that you have the prerogative as a parent to define the rules of the relationship.

If no adult to whom your child is related lives within easy driving distance or if your child's grandparents and aunts and uncles are deceased, strive to find an adult with whom your child can spend time. It may be through a Big Brothers or Big Sisters program. It may be through your church. It may be a neighbor.

Your child needs to hear opinions from other adults who love him. He needs to see how other adults handle various circumstances and situations in life.

An Exception to the Rule The only time you should cut off a relationship between your child and another adult is if you suspect that abuse of any type is occurring—physical, sexual, or emotional. In those cases, cut off the relationship definitively. If your child truly is being abused, he will be grateful to you for rescuing him.

If the child is older at the time of the abuse, let your child know why you no longer are giving your permission for him to spend time with the adult in question. If your child truly has been abused, he will thank you and think better of you.

In sharing your child with others, from time to time, talk over with the other adult various problems your child may be having. Get their insights.

Let some visits be spontaneous, others planned. Keep the relationship as normal as possible. For example, don't insist that your child always dress in her best church or party clothes to visit Aunt Lou.

Maintain Healthy Detachment Don't attempt to debrief your child after each visit. Express your interest in what your child "got to do" with the other adult, but don't grill your child for details beyond what your child is willing to share. The parent who seeks desperately for information sends a message to the child, "I'm not sure I trust you with this adult. I'm not sure I trust her love for you."

Finally, let your child know that it's OK for him to love someone else. You can say to your child, "I'm glad you have such a good relationship with Gramps." Or, "Isn't it neat that Aunt Karen lives close to us so you can be with her?"

One of the greatest qualities about love is that we human beings can never get enough of the real thing. Share your child with others so that he or she can be *deluged* with a massive, overwhelming, outpouring of love. Your child will love being loved like that!

41 ✦ Leave an After-School Love Message for Your Child

Anticipate your child's return after a long day at school. Have a surprise awaiting him. Send the message to your child, "I love being with you. I'm glad you're home!"

Here are some surprises children love:

- *A snack.* I have never met a child who didn't come home from school hungry. Core and cut up an apple. Have half a sandwich ready and waiting, along with a glass of milk. Put out a couple of cookies with a glass of juice.
- *A different kind of treat.* Your message of love may be a new video for your child to play until you get home. It may be a game, an item of clothing that your child has wanted, or an envelope with your child's allowance in it.
- *A note from you.* Stick it on the bathroom mirror: "Glad to see you are at home safe and sound! I'll be home about 5:30 today." Or put a note on the refrigerator door, "There's a piece of cake already cut and wrapped for you as a snack. Not a bite more. Love, Mom."

- *A message on the family answering machine.*
  Parker leaves a message every day for his son
  on their answering machine. His son knows to
  check the machine as soon as he gets home.
  "Hi, son. This is Dad. I'll be home soon. Get
  your homework done now so we can play a little
  catch when I get home. I should be there by six
  o'clock."
- *A phone call from you.* Carolyn calls her son every day at the time he usually gets home. They
  talk over the day for a few minutes, and also the
  family's plans for the evening. Kitt, on the other
  hand, has her son call her the minute *he* gets
  home.

In leaving a message for your child, make certain
that your instructions are clear. Communicate using
words that your child can read. Make certain that
you give *all* the details. For example, tell the child
precisely what time you expect him to come in from
playing basketball, exactly when you'd like for him to
put the casserole in the oven and at what temperature (and remind him to turn on the oven), which
outfit you want him to change into.

The ideal, of course, is for parents to be at home
when their children are at home. In today's world,
that isn't always possible. Make sure that your child
has a "piece of your presence" even if you can't be
there.

42 ✦ Help Your Child Build a Collection

A collection, built over time, is a great way of expressing the continuity of your love to your child.

Sharing Time Whenever possible, choose collections that can relate to *time* you spend with your child. Make a collection not only something that your child *has,* but something your child *does.* Some possibilities are:

- *A stamp collection.* Accompany your child to stamp stores. Take him to the post office when new issues are available.
- *A book collection.* Don't just give your child an occasional volume. Take your child with you to the bookstore to pick out a new addition to his or her "set."
- *A rock or shell collection.* Collect some samples on your hikes together and purchase other items in specialty shops.

A collection may have practical use later in life. In my case, the collection was one of miniature vases. My mother advised that I collect something that I might enjoy even as an adult, and I now often use these little vases for individual blooms around the house or at individual place settings for dinner parties. The vases were acquired as we traveled together rather extensively during my growing-up years.

Building Memories Katie has an add-a-pearl necklace that her parents started for her when she was born. The final pearls on the strand were a present to her on the eve of her wedding, so that she might wear a completed necklace with her wedding gown.

Justin's collection of train cars grows in value for him every year. He has a train set that is the envy of his entire neighborhood. Jordan's collection of Christmas ornaments is something she will take with her when she leaves home one day. Linda's collection of clowns now fills an entire shelf in her room. Clowns still make her smile.

A collection says to your child, "My love extends over time. So does your acquiring of these things. My love for you is longstanding. It grows each day. My love is a treasure of exceedingly great value; just as these things become more valuable to you as time passes, so will my love." Children are here-and-now creatures. As children grow, they have a sense of time, history, and continuity. Let a collection be a tangible expression of your love in the context of years.

43 ✦ Avail Yourself of Help When Your Child Needs It

Don't think that you need to be all things to your child. Get professional help for your child when he needs it. Most parents readily take their children to physicians, dentists, and optometrists. They know they aren't capable of handling certain health care problems. These same parents, however, are often reluctant to get help in areas where they think they are supposed to have the answers.

Learning Problems   Get help when your child needs *tutoring in a school subject.* Don't let your child flounder in a basic subject. If your child isn't reading at grade level or is having trouble with math, get a tutor. Don't let the problem build. I encountered a student in a college classroom one day who stated in a matter-of-fact tone, "I can't do this assignment because I can't do percentages." "OK," I responded. "I'll show you how to figure percentages." "No," she added, "you don't understand. I *can't* do percentages. I've tried for years and I can't *do* them."

This young woman had been "helped" by her father, who, unfortunately, didn't know how to figure percentages either! He had so confused his daughter that he had led her to the conclusion that she was ignorant and totally beyond help in this area of mathematics.

If your child is in tears (or near them) because he or she can't seem to understand a school subject, take tests, or solve a problem—get help. Your child may have received some incorrect or confusing instruction that needs to be undone. Or, he may have a learning disability that needs remediation.

Behavioral Problems   If your child has continued and persistent difficulty dealing with anger, appears despondent and talks about death, can't seem to make or sustain friendships, frequently is in trouble at school, or appears increasingly withdrawn —seek out professional help.

You may want to start with a pastor, rabbi, or priest. You may want to start with your child's teacher, principal, or school counselor. They may refer you elsewhere. If they do, follow up on their lead.

Don't assume that your child will just "grow out of it." He may not. Your child may have had an experience that you know nothing about. He may have been abused in some way or have witnessed abuse. She may have experienced a hurt that she can't tell you about, for any one of a hundred reasons. Give your child the opportunity to talk to a professional counselor about the problem.

Encourage your child. Let your child know that you believe things are going to get better for her!

Above all, restate your love. Say, *"Honey, I love you and I want to see you experience life to the fullest. I want to see you get the greatest amount of fulfillment and enjoyment out of life. At times we all face problems that seem humongous to us. Usually, we find those problems seem smaller if we get somebody to help us with them."* Don't let your child see therapy as a punishment for her behavior; don't let her regard herself as sick or deficient. Put therapy in the context of learning and helping.

Many times parents assume that love will cover all problems or that love will cure all ailments. That isn't so. Many times a problem is related to depths of grief or guilt or loneliness that love can't resolve by itself. A child's physical chemistry may be out of whack, and the root of a learning or behavioral problem may be physiological more than psychological. Your child may have had an encounter or be experiencing something that is completely foreign to your previous experience.

Get the help your child needs. That is often the way in which love manifests itself with greatest impact. "Mom cared enough to help me through this. Dad loved me enough to recognize my need and to get help in meeting it."

44 ✦ Have Something of Your Child's as a Permanent Part of Your Home

This "simple way" is addressed to those grandparents, aunts and uncles, and godparents who frequently have the children they love over to their homes. Here is a way for *you* to say "I love you" to a special child in your life.

Have something in your home that is the child's property, exclusively for his use and available to him whenever he comes to visit. It may be a pillow, blanket, or sheets just for the child's use, or a special towel in the bathroom cupboard, or a bottom dresser drawer filled with a variety of toys, games, and puzzles. That sends a message to your beloved child, "Just as you have a special place in my heart, you have a special place in my home."

Reserved Property Connie has Mickey Mouse sheets available in her linen closet exclusively for the use of her young grandson, Thompson, who comes to spend the night at least once a month. The sheets not only have become a tradition in Thompson's life, but they are a reminder of a happy day spent with his grandparents at Disneyland.

Make sure your child's special items don't go home with your child. This does not mean, of course, that you can't give your child items to take home. A collection of pretty leaves gathered from your autumn-laced sidewalk, flowers from your garden, a batch of homemade cookies, the T-shirt you've painted together. Let your child take away the temporary remembrances of his or her visit.

Special Necessities Have a toothbrush, baby shampoo, and a bottle of bubble bath available exclusively for your child's use. As your child grows into a teen, update the shampoo and add a razor. Your teen will still need a toothbrush and enjoy a bottle of bubble bath or bath salts.

Keep his or her favorite cereal in an airtight plastic container in the cupboard. That goes for all ages. Have a bathrobe and slippers just for your child's use. Keep a nightgown or pajamas at your house for the spur-of-the-moment overnight visit.

Let your child know, "I've planned for you in my life. I want you always to feel comfortable here. I want this to be your home-away-from-home."

45 ✦ Set Rules

Children need and want rules. They need rules for their safety and protection. They also need to know that you are *concerned* with their safety and protection. In spite of what they may say in a moment of anger or frustration, a child regards rules as a sign that you care. Rules say to your child, "I love you enough to care what happens to you. I love you enough to protect you."

When you give your child rules you are not only setting boundaries beyond which they may not go, but you are establishing an area in which they may move with a great deal of freedom. In defining for your child what is off-limits, you are also establishing what is permissible.

Place your emphasis on the positive side of the boundary line when you give rules to your child. Instead of saying, "You may not leave the upper floor of the mall," try saying, "You may go into any store you choose on the upper floor. But, don't go to any other floor before we talk about it."

Here are three guidelines for setting rules:

- Don't let your child engage in any activity that has a high percentage of likelihood for physical or emotional harm.

- Don't let your child willfully destroy property.
- Don't let your child willfully hurt another person.

Sometimes you may want to couch rules in terms of their being "house rules." In other words, let your child know that while certain rules are not the law of the land or principles by which the cosmos operates, they *are* rules that you've decided to have for your house and for your family.

As a parent, making rules *is* your prerogative. Let your child know that you have the privilege of making rules. As long as you have responsibility for your child, you have the right to make rules for his behavior and to require that he keep them.

Use Your Instinct Still other rules are what a friend of mine terms "instinct rules." Rules tend to govern generalities. Children tend to deal in specifics. Applying general rules to specific situations often comes down to "instinct." You can always say to your child, "My instinct as a father tells me this is one time when I should say no." Or, "I know your regular curfew is eleven o'clock. And yes, it's true that on a few occasions I've let you extend that to midnight. But this time the eleven o'clock rule needs to stand. And no, I don't have any other reason than that I have a feeling that you should be in by eleven."

You don't need to explain all of your rules to your child. Some you will want to explain. Explain what you feel needs to be known or that which a child can understand. It is your privilege as a parent, however, to require obedience even without an explanation. Let your child know up front that "just because I said so" *is* an acceptable answer in many situations.

Be Consistent   The most important aspect of a rule is its consistent application. Don't switch rules in the middle of the stream. Let Monday's rule also be Tuesday's rule. Also, be consistent in your rules for all your children. Don't have one set of rules for the boys and another for the girls.

Rules need to flow from a consistent value system. If it is wrong to lie to parents, it also should be wrong to lie to a brother or sister. If it is wrong to cheat on a test, it also should be wrong to cheat when you are counting out Monopoly money to your friends.

Be Sensitive to Your Child   Be aware that in many cases your child wants you to say no. He doesn't want to be responsible for a yes decision. The movie is guaranteed to frighten every viewer out of his wits. All the other kids are going. Your child pleads with you in their presence for permission to go. You say, "No." Don't be surprised if your child appears relieved.

Be sensitive to an adjustment of rules as your child grows up. The rule of lights out at eight o'clock is not going to be pertinent to a twelve-year-old.

Rules imply a set of punishments. There has to be an "if" clause for most rules to have impact. *"If you leave the yard, you will have to come into the house and stay inside for the rest of the afternoon." "If you hit Marsha again, accidentally or not, you will have a ten-minute 'time out' when we get home."*

Always, always, *always* state rules in terms that children understand. Use simple, concise language. Spell out consequences clearly.

Be prepared to restate and restate and restate your position. Tuesday's rule may be Monday's rule, but your child may not remember it was a rule or that it is Tuesday! As my friend Charles once said to me, "Most of parenting seems to come down to one word: repetition."

Follow through on punishments when your established rules are disobeyed. Don't make idle threats. Let your child know that when you say something, you mean it. Let your child know that your decision is final and not subject to negotiation. That way, your child will be more likely to believe you when you say, "I love you!"

46 ✦ Pray for Your Child

Earlier in this book, we provided suggestions for praying *with* your child. Another way to love your child is to pray *for* your child.

Prayer does something within your own heart. It enlarges your capacity to feel love for your child. It brings things to your conscious mind that may have been lingering in your subconscious. It provides an avenue for you to forgive yourself for times when you know that you have failed your child as a loving parent.

Sabrina often goes into her son's room to pray for him while he is away at school. There in the midst of all his "junk," surrounded by the environment he has created largely for himself, she will lie on his bed and attempt to see the world as her son sees it. "I get a much better sense of what he values and what he's facing," she says. "It's as if I'm truly 'walking a mile in his moccasins.'"

Occasions for Prayer

- Pray for your child before you punish your child. Ask God for guidance, temperance, and patience.

- Pray for wisdom that you might help your child confront life's problems and that you might train your child in the best ways possible.
- Pray for forgiveness for those times when you know that you've let your child down in some way.
- Pray for a solution to your child's problems. It may be a behavioral problem, a health problem, a school problem.
- Pray for the ability to show more love to your child.
- Pray a blessing on your child. Ask God for an abundant outpouring of opportunities and good things into your child's life, both now and in the future.

You'll find that prayer brings your relationship with your child into sharper focus, that you have more patience and insight into your child's life, and that you have an added sense of strength as a parent.

Your child will know you are praying for him. There will be times when he overhears you and you aren't even aware of it. There will be times when he wants you to pray for him in his presence, especially if he is sick or facing a challenge of some type.

Let your child know that you are praying for him. Ask him, from time to time (or even daily) if there is something in his life about which he would like for you to pray.

A Bedtime Ritual   Jim sometimes found it difficult to talk to his children face to face about serious matters. In fact, Jim didn't talk much at all in the presence of his family members. All of his life he had been classified as shy or reserved. It was a fact his wife and children accepted.

Instead of carrying on conversations with his children, Jim had a habit of going into their rooms after they were asleep, and there, staring over the side of the crib or sitting on the edge of the bed, he would pray for his children, one by one. He would tell them how he felt, and what he hoped for them. He would pray for their future and their success in life.

Pray for your child in his presence:

- When your child is sick. Let him know that you believe he is going to get well.
- When your child is lonely or sad. Let him know that you believe he's going to have bright moments ahead.
- When your child is facing a real challenge—moral, academic, athletic, spiritual. Let your child know that you believe he is going to stand strong and come through this challenge victoriously and that even if he doesn't win, he can still be a "winner."

Nobody truly understands how prayer works. But nearly everybody can attest to a time when a prayer was answered. Prayer fills in the gaps that you may feel in your relationship with your child.

47 ✦ Don't Forget the Little Touches

Let your relationship with your child be filled with easygoing, not-too-serious, little touches.

Give him a little shoulder hug as you stand in the supermarket check-out line, hold her hand for just thirty seconds as you walk from the car into church, squeeze his hand after a blessing is asked before the evening meal.

Parting Rituals Help Brad absolutely refused to let his mother hug or kiss him goodbye as he left for school. "What if the guys see you?" he would say. "They'd think I'm a sissy." Instead, Brad and his mother share "elbow kisses." As Brad leaves in the morning, he puts out his elbow toward his mother, she puts out hers, and for just a second or two, they touch elbows. Subtle. Not too mushy. But a little touch that marks every day.

Jeremy's mother drives him to school each day. Their parting ritual is similar. Mom simply reaches over and squeezes his knee three times. "One for me, one for Dad, and one for God." Jeremy feels three times loved.

Marlene and her mother hold fingers. "When Marlene was just a toddler, she'd reach up and grab hold of my little finger. She didn't want me to hold her hand—I think that was too much of *my* holding *her* hand. Instead, she wanted the independence she felt in grasping *my* finger at will. Sometimes when we are standing in church together now (and she's already to my shoulder, you realize), I'll still find her reaching over to link her little finger with mine."

Grandfather offers his arm to Mindy as a gallant gesture every time they walk together. Mindy feels special as "Grandfather's girl." (Grandfather also feels more secure in walking.)

Little Touches Mean a Lot What do these moments of touching do for your child?

- They remind him of your presence. A small touch can be reassuring to a child just before he goes on stage, or as he comes or goes from your presence. If a child is standing close enough to you for you to touch him, consider him within touching range.
- Little touches remind your child that you think she is *worthy* of your touch, that you want to be close to her, and that you enjoy her company.
- Little touches communicate, *"Thanks, honey."* Or, *"Way to go."* Or, *"You can do it."* And always, *"I love you."*

Don't make them a major production. Keep them as *little* touches, a layer of icing on the rich cake of your love!

48 ✦ Let Your Child Know He Can Hurt You

When your child hurts your feelings, willfully or unknowingly, let your child know that you have been hurt. Find a moment when the two of you are alone and say, *"Honey, you remember when you said [or did, or didn't do] . . . well, that hurt me."*

Your child is likely to sense that you have been hurt, although he may not define it as hurt. He may think you are angry, upset, frustrated, or annoyed. By telling your child you have been hurt, you teach him to understand your feelings and to be more sensitive to various signals from others in the future.

Telling your child that you have been hurt gives your child an opportunity to ask your forgiveness. He may not use words, he may just be kinder to you for a few days or show up with a flower or write you a little note. Accept your child's acts of repentance.

Legitimate hurts which you should discuss with your child include any incident when your child shows disrespect for you:

- Insults (public or private).
- Cursing or name-calling, at you or about you.
- Lies told about you.

- Blatant and willful rejection.
- Nagging criticism.

In some cases, your child's behavior may warrant punishment from you. How can you tell when punishment is warranted? Any time your child does something to you that you don't want your child to do to any other adult, including his or her own spouse someday.

In cases where you decide punishment is necessary, let your child know plainly *before* you punish him, *"I've been very hurt by what you've just done or said, but that is not the reason that I'm punishing you. I'm punishing you because that is not an acceptable way to treat any adult, including me. I don't want you ever to do that again. This punishment is to help you remember not to repeat such behavior."*

Draw a distinction between your personal hurt and your parental role as the punishment-giver. Assure your child that, in spite of your hurt feelings, your love for him remains strong.

Positive Messages   What messages are sent to your child when you let him know that he can, and has, hurt you?

First, he will learn that your love is resilient. It can survive injury and insult. It can last through rejection. It can endure beyond criticism. *"My love for you, honey, is stronger than anything you can throw up against it."*

Second, she will learn that loving relationships are

not marked by insult, hurt, criticism, or lies. Instead, the hallmarks of loving relationships are praise, giving, blessing, helping, and truth.

Third, your child will learn that his actions can wound and that he is responsible for the wounds he inflicts on others. Children often see adults as impervious to hurt. (They often see God in this way, too.) Letting your child know that you are vulnerable makes your child more sensitive to the fact that all human beings have feelings that can be injured.

Emotional Growth   Many children grow up thinking, "It's not my fault if another person feels hurt. It's their fault. They shouldn't have felt that way. They should have been able to overlook what I said or should have ignored what I did." That's a self-centered, self-justifying, arrogant attitude that often results in shallow, temporary, unsatisfying, or dysfunctional relationships.

Confront your child with the insults that issue from his mouth. He is just as responsible for what he says as for what he does.

Loving relationships sometimes do have painful moments. Don't deny them. Grow through them. If you didn't love, you wouldn't feel pain. When your child causes you pain, show your child that love can conquer or outlive pain. Show your child just how strong love can be. He'll never know it if he thinks that he can never hurt you.

49 ✦ Personalize Your Child's World

Lift up your child's name. Let him know that you consider his name, the nearest and dearest representations of himself beyond his own physical body, to be valuable beyond measure. You will be sending a loud and clear message to your child, "I count you as special. I love you as I love no other."

Encourage your child to stick his hands and feet into the wet cement poured adjacent to your new swimming pool. Date it. Give your child the thrill of knowing that he has made a lasting mark on your home.

Monogram a couple of your teen's long-sleeved dress shirts. It only costs a few dollars at a tailor shop. Send the message to your child that he is special and that you consider him a cut above the norm.

Personalize Your Child's Room Have a nameplate made for your child's room. It might be an engraved brass door knocker for the door into his room. It might be a name carved out of wood. It might be a needlework nameplate. Let your child know with assurity: "This is my space. My name and my space are important to Mom and Dad."

Frame certificates for your child's room in which

his name is associated with a good deed. Show his trophies. Does your child fail to win trophies or bring home certificates? Then make up one for him. Buy one for him. It can be a certificate awarded to "The Greatest Daughter in the World" or for "Superior Performance as a Son." Trophy shops have all sorts of toppers and styles. I recently saw a trophy in the room of a thirteen-year-old boy that read, "Grandpa's Favorite Fishing Companion—Summer 1988" above the child's name.

How about ordering a monogrammed pin for your teenage daughter or having her first initial engraved on a locket? How about monogramming a beach towel or oversized bath towel for your son?

More Personal Touches

- Buy a mug with your child's initial on it.
- Put her initials on a diary or journaling book.
- Have your child's initials put on his first leather wallet.
- Buy a keychain with your child's initial after she gets her first driver's license.

These added touches tell your child, "You are unique. Even if someone else in the world has your name, nobody else by that name is *my* child. And, nobody else receives the same love that I have in my heart for you."

50 ✦ Take Time for Yourself

Be good to yourself. Pamper yourself occasionally. Send a signal to your child that you like yourself. The more valuable you consider yourself to be, the more valuable are your expressions of love to your child.

Do you think of yourself as being important? You are! You are your child's parent. That's important. Hold your head up and declare to yourself in the mirror, "I have an important role to fill on this earth." Let your child sense the feeling, "I'm loved by an important person."

Do you think of yourself as being beautiful? You are to your child. Nothing is more beautiful than the touch of your hands, your smile, the twinkle in your eye, and your arms wrapped around your child in a bear hug. Send a message to your child that she is adored by a wonderful, lovely person.

Respect yourself. Your child will not only have greater respect for you, but also greater respect for the love you share.

Love Yourself Make it a habit to get dressed, comb your hair, and put on your makeup before your child leaves the house in the morning. Shut yourself away from time to time to take a long bubble bath.

Simply say to your child, "Excuse me while I take a moment for luxury. You know the house rules. Keep them."

Dress up for dinner occasionally, and insist that your children dress up, too. This is especially important if your spouse comes home dressed in a suit—and perhaps, heels!

Share It with Your Child   Share your accomplishments with your child, too. Let your child know when you win an award, receive praise from a supervisor, or are pleased within yourself at the good job you've done on a project. *"It was a smashing dinner, if I do say so myself!" "It was first-rate work, whether the big boss ever sees it or not."*

Occasionally declare a household naptime or quiet hour. If your child complains that he isn't sleepy, let him curl up on his bed with a book. Instruct him, *"Don't awaken me, and don't leave your room!"* Let your child know that you deserve a little time and space to call your own, including an occasional nap.

Enjoy the purchase of a new dress, suit, or pair of shoes. Delight in gifts of fragrance and personal items. Let your child know that you value your own body, your appearance, your accomplishments.

The more your child senses that you value yourself, the greater the value your child will place upon you. And the greater he will value your expressions of love.

51 ✦ Protect Your Child

As a parent, you are your child's foremost protector. Parents often have a good understanding of that when their children are young. *"Don't run into the street." "Don't touch the hot stove." "Don't talk to strangers."* The responsibility increases, however, rather than decreases as your child grows older.

- *Protect your child from physical danger.* Make sure your child knows when and how to make an emergency call. Make certain your child knows his name, address, phone number, your name, and your phone number at work. Prepare your child for encounters with strangers. *"If anybody offers you anything that sounds too good to be true, run like crazy and come tell me about it!"*

  Rehearse fire drills with your child in your own home. Teach your child what to do if he gets lost. Give your child swimming lessons. Teach your child basic first-aid skills. Above all, make sure your child *feels* safe in his own home. You may need to add another lock to the back door.
- *Protect your child from drugs.* Give him the infor-

mation he needs, and give it to him before anybody else does. Arm yourself with facts. Explain
the difference between medicines and illegal
drugs to your child. Let your child know that
drugs abuse people and take control of their
lives.

- *Protect your child from an unwanted pregnancy.*
Talk to your child about sex before anybody
else does. Explain how both the male and fe-
male bodies function. Talk about appropriate be-
haviors between boys and girls, men and
women, according to your value system. Don't
just say, "Don't." Tell your child why. Discuss
precautions, prevention, and abstinence. Ex-
plode the myths that your child is likely to hear
about sex. Say to your child, *"I love you so much
that I want you to experience all of the right kinds
of love at the right time and in the right ways."*

- *Protect your child's mind.* Don't allow pornogra-
phy in your home. Watch what your child
watches. Do you see occultic signs or practices?
(Do you know what to look for? If not, find out.)
Do you see violence? Do you see blatant acts of
prejudice against race, sex, or nationality? Turn
off the message.

    Guide your child's selection of reading mate-
rial. Regulate your child's attendance at movies.
Feed your child's mind as well as you feed your
child's body.

- *Protect your child from abuse.* Let your child
know that he has a right *not* to be abused physi-

cally, emotionally, or sexually. Tell your child in plain terms what is off limits, what is private about his or her body, and how to recognize an emotionally destructive relationship. Reinforce the message to your child, *"I love you and don't want to see you abused in any way."*

Do not allow self-abusive behavior in which a child calls himself a failure, declares that he is inadequate in some way, or inflicts an injury on himself. Assure him you will continue to love him even if he never hits a home run. Tell her you will always love her, even if she never gets her hair to do exactly what she wants it to do. Continually reinforce the message to your child, "I love you for who you are, not for anything that you do or don't do."

- *Protect your child's heart.* Give your child lessons in how to cope with failure or rejection. Teach your child how to stand up on the side of moral right. Give your child a faith to which he can cling in dark, lonely, or frightening moments. Say to your child, *"I love you and I want you to love yourself."*

❤ Afterword

What we've tried to do in this book is to create more ways to bring love to a sometimes loveless world. We hope you will use our ideas to tell all of the special people in your life how much they mean to you.

Mother Teresa has aptly said that people in America are dying (spiritually) from emotional hunger. We Americans have the resources to end this emotional famine. Three short words spoken sincerely have the power to satisfy our craving. Those three words are "I love you."